THE PASSION PROJECT PLAYBOOK

A STEP-BY-STEP GUIDE TO LAUNCHING YOUR ONLINE BUSINESS AT ANY AGE

DOUG KALUNIAN

LOOKING AHEAD: YOUR ROADMAP TO EN-TREPRENEURSHIP

As you explore 'The Passion Project Playbook,' you'll find practical guidance to transform your passions, interests, or skills into a thriving business.

Tailored for professionals over 50, this book empowers you to explore new horizons by blending your past experiences with newfound enthusiasm.

Here's a glimpse of what lies ahead in the upcoming chapters:

- **Chapter 1**: Embracing the Add-On and Encore Entrepreneur: Explore the concept of starting a business later in life, uncovering the potential for personal fulfillment and financial stability through passion-driven ventures.

- **Chapter 2:** Discovering Your Passion: Uncover how to align your passions with market needs and personal strengths. This chapter offers practical self-reflection techniques to help you pinpoint what excites you and holds potential as a successful side business.

- **Chapter 3:** Building the Foundation of Your Business: Learn the essential steps to legally register and structure your business. This chapter provides practical advice for creating a solid foundation, ensuring your side hustle operates smoothly and efficiently.

- **Chapter 4:** Navigating the Tech Terrain: Overcome tech challenges and harness AI-powered tools to your advantage. Whether you're a tech novice or an expert, this chapter provides guidance on leveraging modern technologies to strengthen your online business presence.

- **Chapter 5:** Mastering Online Marketing: Unlock strategies for effective digital marketing. Learn to craft engaging content and leverage social media to create a strong online brand that connects with your target audience.

- **Chapter 6:** Crafting a Winning Launch Plan: Develop a launch plan that sets your business on a path for success. This chapter guides you in understanding your audience and using pre-launch marketing strategies to generate excitement.

- **Chapter 7**: Overcoming Newbie Challenges: Tackle common obstacles faced by new entrepreneurs. Gain valuable insights into building resilience and honing problem-solving skills to keep your venture on course.

- **Chapter 8**: Financing Your Passion Project: Discover creative and strategic ways to finance your side hustle while maintaining financial stability. This chapter explores budgeting techniques and potential funding sources to support your entrepreneurial goals.

- **Chapter 15:** Aligning Vision with Progress: Align your business objectives with your personal goals. Explore strategies to adapt to changing circumstances while remaining true to your overarching vision.

- **Chapter 16**: Empowerment for a Brighter Future: Celebrate your transformative journey, armed with the knowledge and inspiration to transform your passions into profits and create a fulfilling future.

- **Chapter 17:** Epilogue: Reflect on the themes of passion, innovation, and courage. Embrace your unique abilities, leverage digital tools, and build meaningful connections to create a business aligned with your vision. Be inspired to take the first steps toward transforming dreams into reality, unlocking endless possibilities for a fulfilling entrepreneurial journey.

Each chapter builds upon the previous one, guiding you step-by-step from introspection to action, ensuring your journey into entrepreneurship is both informed and inspiring

CONTENTS

INTRODUCTION

Welcome to a journey where your passions and dreams converge in the exciting world of online entrepreneurship.

Have you ever wondered how to turn what you love into a profitable side hustle? If so, you're in the right place.

"The Passion Project Playbook" offers you insights and strategies to help you turn your passion into profits, all while navigating the exciting and sometimes overwhelming realm of online business.

Think of this as your personal roadmap, crafted for first-time entrepreneurs brimming with hope, passion, and the excitement of new challenges and adventures.

Starting something new can be daunting, but every successful entrepreneur begins the same way: with a simple idea and a lot of heart.

That's where this book steps in: to guide you from those uncertain first steps to a place of clarity, confidence, and meaningful action.

This book is here to empower you with the knowledge and confidence needed to take those first bold steps.

Picture waking up each day, excited to work—not out of obligation, but driven by passion.

Imagine leveraging technology to connect with a global audience, sharing what you love, and earning an income from it.

This isn't just a dream—it's a reality waiting for you to seize it.

Together, we'll explore practical tools and strategies, embrace learning curves with a smile, and navigate the challenges and triumphs of building a business from scratch.

If you're ready to embark on a new adventure, this book will equip you with the tools, strategies, and mindset to succeed. Armed with enthusiasm and a willingness to learn, let's begin this exciting journey together.

Open these pages and embark on a journey of limitless potential and creative freedom.

Welcome to your entrepreneurial journey, where your unique vision transforms into reality, paving the way for both prosperity and meaningful impact on your life and on the lives of others.

CHAPTER 1

EMBRACING THE ADD-ON AND ENCORE ENTREPRENEUR TRANSFORMING PASSION INTO PROFIT

Julia Child discovered her passion for cooking later in life, embarking on a transformative culinary journey during her time in Paris—a journey that would redefine her career and bring joy to millions.

Though initially lacking formal training, Julia immersed herself in French cooking, studying at Le Cordon Bleu.

At age 49, she channeled her passion into the iconic cooking Mastering the Art of French Cooking, revolutionizing American kitchens.

At age 51, Julia introduced America to cooking shows through her groundbreaking program, The French Chef.

The show elevated her public profile, solidifying her status as a beloved culinary educator, and leaving an enduring impact on American cooking culture.

Her story demonstrates how a passion discovered later in life can lead to a fulfilling and highly impactful career.

Similarly inspiring is Vera Wang, who transitioned into the world of bridal fashion design at age 40, following a distinguished career as a fashion editor.

Inspired by her own bridal experience, Wang discovered and filled a gap in the market for elegant, innovative wedding designs. Her creations quickly gained recognition, cementing her status as a global icon in bridal fashion.

Vera's journey highlights the potential to reinvent oneself by leveraging personal experiences and professional skills into a thriving creative enterprise.

Our third example is a woman who had been involved in catering and lifestyle-oriented projects over the years.

Yet, it wasn't until later in life that she fully developed her passions for cooking, entertaining, and homemaking into a hugely successful multimedia empire.

Who was this?

Martha Stewart, who at 50, founded Martha Stewart Living Omnimedia.

Her brand evolved into a multimedia empire, encompassing television shows, magazines, and online content—demonstrating that it's never too late to turn passion into profit.

All three successful entrepreneurs, Julia Child, Vera Wang, and Martha Stewart, exemplify the remarkable results of pursuing passions and turning them into profitable ventures.

Their stories remind us that it's never too late to reinvent ourselves. For those entering the next phase of life, a side hustle offers the perfect opportunity to transform personal passions into professional pursuits.

As you reflect on these stories, consider how your passions could spark a similar transformation—bringing fulfillment, financial security, and entrepreneurial success in your 40s, 50s, and beyond.

WHY SIDE HUSTLES MATTER AFTER 50

At this stage in life, a side hustle transcends the pursuit of extra income; it's a pathway to emotional fulfillment, financial independence, and a renewed sense of purpose.

Picture a life where you wake up energized, pursuing what truly fulfills you while securing your financial future at the same time.

For many, career stagnation or the reality of dwindling retirement savings trigger concerns about what lies ahead. But this is precisely where side hustles step in, transforming uncertainties into opportunities.

The beauty of side hustles lies in their dual appeal: enriching your life while bolstering your bank account.

These ventures offer a chance to explore new passions or reinvest in old ones, ultimately providing a sense of purpose and rejuvenation.

Rather than experiencing 50 as a plateau, view it as a launchpad—a chance to align your daily activities with what genuinely excites you.

For those wary of venturing into the unknown, remember that you're not starting from scratch. You're starting from

experience. Decades of professional and personal exploration equip you with unique skills and insights.

By directing this substantial foundation towards a side hustle, you not only tap into fresh opportunities but also navigate them with wisdom and confidence.

This stage of life, ripe with potential, is a prime time for
change. By embracing side hustles, you can redefine what
success looks like for you, marrying experience with the excitement of new beginnings.

As we embrace the challenges and possibilities that come
with age, the shift towards side hustles not only redefines
personal fulfillment and success but also opens up a landscape rich with trends and opportunities.

In today's dynamic world, leveraging digital platforms and
emerging market trends is crucial for encore entrepreneurs
to unlock their full potential and craft meaningful, impactful ventures.

TRENDS AND OPPORTUNITIES FOR ENCORE ENTRE-
PRENEURS

In today's dynamic economy, people aged 50 and older are
embracing 'encore entrepeneurship—a growing movement driven by the accessibility of digital tools and a cultural shift toward lifelong learning and flexibility. This environment offers unprecedented opportunities for new
business ventures.

It's fascinating to see how many professionals over 50 are
diving into entrepreneurship lately.

According to the Bureau of Labor Statistics, there's been a huge jump in numbers. From 2000 to 2020, the number of self-employed people aged 55-64 shot up by 140%, and those 65 and older rose by 110%.

Clearly, the idea of starting a business isn't just for the young—it's catching on with older adults too!

The Small Business Administration notes that businesses started by older entrepreneurs have greater longevity than those launched by younger entrepreneurs..

A 2019 Guidant Financial survey of over 2,600 entrepreneurs, published on SCORE.org, supports these trends.

They found that 67% of entrepreneurs over age 50 report that their businesses are making a profit.

They also found that 64% of entrepreneurs over age 50 report that they plan to expand their current businesses!

It seems like all that experience and those networks they've built over the years are playing to their advantage.

And let's not forget the digital side of things.

The Pew Research Center notes that internet and smartphone use among older adults has grown significantly.

This means they can easily tap into online platforms for marketing and engagement.

This growing digital presence is essential for building brand recognition and fostering customer connections in today's marketplace.

All these numbers highlight that older adults are becoming a powerhouse in the business arena, using their passions, know-how and online savvy to make a real impact.

While these statistics focus on the broader trend, they definitely show that creating a strong online presence is vital for anyone looking to succeed in business today.

Success as an encore entrepreneur lies in embracing digital tools and staying attuned to evolving market trends.

The following resources demonstrate how you can bridge your professional experience with today's digital opportunities to thrive as an entrepreneur.

LEVERAGING DIGITAL TOOLS

The digital landscape offers numerous platforms to simplify the entrepreneurial process:

E-Commerce Platforms:

- Platforms like Shopify, Stan Store, SamCart, and Etsy are tools that provide easy-to-use interfaces for setting up online shops.

- They enable entrepreneurs to reach a global customer base without the overhead of a physical store.

Social Media Marketing:

- Harness the potential of social media platforms like Facebook, Instagram, and YouTube for marketing and community building.

- These platforms are effective for showcasing your products and engaging directly with customers, creating loyal communities.

TAPPING INTO PROFESSIONAL EXPERIENCE

Your vast professional experience is a rich resource for consultancy or educational endeavors:

Freelance Platforms:

- Sites like Fiverr, ProFinder, and Upwork offer multiple providers of specialized services, reaching a broad audience seeking expertise in various fields.

Educational Content Creation:

- Platforms such as Teachable allow you to create and sell courses or webinars, turning your knowledge into a profitable venture, while also enriching others.

Understanding Market Trends

Staying informed about market trends and evolving consumer demands helps your business remain competitive and posed for growth.

It's not just about keeping up—it's about staying ahead.

Keeping abreast of market dynamics ensures your business remains relevant and competitive:

Trends Analysis:

- Tools like Google Trends can be instrumental in understanding what consumers are interested in, allowing you to adapt your offerings accordingly.

Eco-Friendly Opportunities:

- With growing consumer interest in sustainability, explore products and services that cater to environmentally conscious customers.

These strategies are not just theoretical but have been successfully employed by many budding entrepreneurs tapping into the wealth of digital resources to help build their audience and grow their businesses.

By doing so, they've not only achieved financial success but have also crafted fulfilling, new career paths that resonate with their passions and principles.

This is your opportunity to utilize these resources and trends to carve out a unique niche in the evolving market.

With the right tools and a keen eye on market trends, the world of encore entrepreneurship beckons with opportunities to innovate and succeed.

Now that you're equipped with insights into leveraging digital tools and market trends, it's time to focus inward.

Defining your personal passions is the first step toward building a business that reflects your aspirations and seizes today's vibrant entrepreneurial opportunities.

DISCOVER YOUR PASSION AND BUILD A BUSINESS

Before diving into the logistics of starting your business, take a moment to reflect on what truly excites and motivates you.

Finding a business idea that aligns your passions with the needs of the world can be transformative. Building a strong foundation starts with gaining clarity about what drives you.

The following exercises are designed to guide you in aligning your passions with opportunities for meaningful and profitable ventures. When your passions align with profitable opportunities, you're not just setting yourself up for success, you're also building something that lasts.

This blend of passion and market savvy keeps you excited and helps you adapt when the going gets rough.

So, dive into these exercises with curiosity and enthusiasm. They're here to help you discover where your interests and the chance to make a difference in the lives of others—and some profit—come together.

EXERCISE #1: PASSION INVENTORY

Why It's Important: The Passion Inventory helps you identify activities that bring you joy and uncover potential business opportunities.

By focusing on what you love, you're more likely to create a venture that not only succeeds but also fulfills you.

Instructions:

1. Settle into the Mindset: Find a quiet space, free from distractions, to focus your thoughts.

2. List Freely: Take 10 minutes to write down activities that bring you joy. Include anything that excites you, from gardening to solving puzzles, without limiting yourself.

3. Identify Core Passions: Circle three activities that stand out the most and reflect on why they resonate with you.

4. Consider Business Potential: Think about how these passions could translate into business opportunities.

For example, if you're passionate about gardening, you could explore opportunities such as designing urban gardens, offering workshops on sustainable living, or starting a blog to share your expertise.

EXERCISE #2: VISUALIZATION AND JOURNALING

Why It's Important: This exercise encourages you to envision your passions as part of your daily life, helping you chart a path toward turning dreams into reality.

Instructions:

1. Create a Quiet Space: Choose a comfortable, distraction-free spot where you can focus.

2. Visualize Your Ideal Day: Close your eyes and picture your ideal workday. What are you doing, and where are you?

3. Journal Your Vision: Spend 15 minutes writing about this ideal day, noting details of tasks, environment, and interactions.

4. Extract Insights: Review your writing to find insights about possible business ventures that resonate with this vision.

Example: Imagine teaching cooking classes in a warm, inviting kitchen and connecting with eager learners. This vision could lead to hosting online workshops or creating video tutorials.

EXERCISE #3: MIND MAPPING

Why It's Important: Mind Mapping helps you delve into a single passion, uncovering a variety of potential business opportunities tied to your interests.

Instructions:

1. Select a Passion: Choose one passion from your inventory that you feel strongly about.

2. Center Your Mind Map: Write this passion in the center of a blank page and circle it.

3. Branch Out Ideas: Around the central circle, jot down related skills, ideas, or opportunities, connecting them like a web.

4. Evaluate Possibilities: For each secondary idea, ask yourself how you might create products or services from these.

Example: If cooking is your central passion, your mind map might include visions of creating a cookbook, hosting online cooking classes, or starting a food blog.

These connections could inspire you to combine them into a dynamic food-focused enterprise.

Approach these exercises with curiosity and excitement.

Remember, they serve not only as stepping stones to channel your passions into a thriving business.

They also act as confidence builders as you discover how your unique talents and passions can become the heart of a successful business.

However, as entrepreneurs start on their journey, most experience a level of fear and uncertainty.

Next, we'll address the common fears associated with starting a new business, and how you can propel yourself forward with assurance and vigor.

FACING FEARS AND MOVING FORWARD

Starting an entrepreneurial journey later in life can feel intimidating. But overcoming common fears is the first step to unlocking your full potential. Let's delve into some common fears and explore practical strategies to navigate them with confidence.

IT'S NEVER TOO LATE TO START

You might wonder: Is it too late for me to start? The answer is a resounding no.

With years of experience and the growing accessibility of online tools, there has never been a better time to turn your dreams into reality. Remember, your wealth of knowledge is a valuable asset that positions you uniquely in your chosen field.

EMBRACING TECHNOLOGY

Another common concern is adapting to new technologies. You may question your ability to learn new digital skills. However, many platforms are designed to be user-friendly, with abundant tutorials and support communities available. Start with small steps—perhaps mastering one tool at a time—and gradually increase your expertise.

TRUSTING YOUR INSTINCTS AND EXPERIENCE

Some budding entrepreneurs fear they might not have the right idea or that their idea isn't viable.

Trust in your instincts and draw on the wealth of experience you've accumulated over the years. For example, consider how your unique perspective or expertise might address a gap in the market. Use feedback from trusted peers and mentors to refine your ideas. Remember, innovation often stems from experience and perspective, both of which you've honed over years. Approach your entrepreneurial journey with confidence and enthusiasm, knowing that every obstacle is a stepping stone to a fulfilling new chapter in life. With tools in hand to uncover your passions, let's look at a couple of inspiring, real-life examples of those who've successfully transformed their ideas into impactful ventures. Discover how individuals like Marci Alboher and Joy Mangano harnessed their passions and skills to embark on successful entrepreneurial journeys, illustrating the transformative power of pursuing what you love.

MARCI ALBOHER: A PIONEER IN ENCORE CAREERS

Marci Alboher's journey from practicing law to becoming a leader in encore entrepreneurship showcases the transformative power of aligning one's passions with purposeful work. Her story is not just about personal reinvention, but about how experience, when repurposed, can lead to profound impact and fulfillment. Marci began her professional life in the demanding arena of law, a field that offered stability but stifled her creative aspirations. The turning point came as she reflected on a growing dissatisfaction with the rigid confines of her career and a burgeoning desire to explore journalism—a field that would allow her to engage dynamically with the world. The decision to leave behind a successful legal career didn't come without its trials.

Marci grappled with the fear of starting from scratch and the uncertainty of success in an entirely different domain. However, she leveraged her skills in analysis and communication, and applied them to her writing endeavors. This transition was marked by a deep dive into freelancing, where she began to establish her voice and reputation. Marci's writings soon earned her recognition, leading to opportunities to write about the very theme that defined her journey: Encore Careers. Her pioneering work, "The Encore Career Handbook," became both a guide and source of inspiration for those looking to pivot their careers in midlife. Through her efforts, Marci addressed the common fears many face—fear of obsolescence, technological challenges, and the daunting task of reinventing oneself.

Marci's path involved several strategic steps:

1. Leveraging Existing Skills: She utilized her analytical prowess and communication skills from her legal background.

2. Expanding Networks: By engaging with communities interested in encore careers, she built connections that enriched her knowledge and impact.

3. Embracing New Mediums: Marci embraced digital tools, blogging, and public speaking, which expanded her reach and authority in the field.

OUTCOMES AND IMPACT

Today, Marci Alboher stands as a mentor to many who seek to redefine success beyond traditional boundaries. Her efforts have not only provided others with actionable pathways to their own encore careers but have also emphasized the importance of purpose-driven work.

KEY LESSONS

For aspiring entrepreneurs, Marci's journey underscores several key lessons:

- Adaptability is Strength: Use your past experiences as a springboard into new ventures.

- Pursue Passion with Purpose: Aligning work with personal passions can lead to deeply fulfilling outcomes.

- Continuous Learning: Embrace growth and learning in new areas, particularly unfamiliar technologies.

Marci's story is a resonant reminder that it's never too late to realign one's career path with what truly excites and fulfills us.

Her legacy is one of encouragement for all who dare to pursue passion over predictability.

Similarly, Joy Mangano took her passion and fought the odds by persistently overcoming challenges to find ultimate success.

Joy Mangano: Inventor and Entrepreneur Extraordinaire

Joy Mangano, a trailblazing American inventor and entrepreneur, rose to fame in her 50s by revolutionizing the marketing and sales of everyday household products.

In her late 30s and early 40s, Joy Mangano was a single mother juggling multiple jobs while determined to improve her family's quality of life. Her breakthrough came with the invention of the 'Miracle Mop,' a self-wringing mop that revolutionized household cleaning by making it faster and easier. The idea emerged from a genuine need she identified in her own life—an easy solution to a cumbersome task.

Launching the Miracle Mop was no easy feat. Joy encountered significant challenges including financial constraints and skepticism in a market dominated by male inventors and business leaders. Determined to bring her invention to the masses, she invested her savings into creating a prototype, and later, she took her product to trade shows and small business meetings to gain traction.

Joy's big break came with her unique insight into leveraging direct consumer engagement. Despite early setbacks, she managed to get a spot on QVC, the television shopping network. Her charismatic and relatable presentation style captivated viewers, transforming the Miracle Mop into an overnight success with over 18,000 units sold during her first appearance on QVC.

Through perseverance, Joy expanded her business, creating additional products such as Huggable Hangers and collaborating with major retail outlets. Her company, Ingenious Designs, became a home-goods empire, eventually selling to the Home Shopping Network (HSN).

Joy Mangano's story highlights several key insights:

- Identifying Market Needs: Base innovations on real, everyday challenges to ensure product relevance and appeal.

- Persistence Pays Off: Overcoming early rejections and challenges can lead to breakthrough success.

- Direct Engagement: Sell directly to consumers when possible to create a personal connection and trust.

Joy's journey from a challenging start to becoming a self-made millionaire exemplifies the power of innovation, determination, and leveraging personal experience and insight, offering a beacon of hope and inspiration for would-be entrepreneurs in their 50s and beyond.

REFLECTIVE QUESTION:

Are you ready to transform your passion into a thriving business and share it with the world?

What will it take for you to get started?

TAKING THE FIRST STEP

As you've observed through the journeys of Julia Child, Vera Wang, Marci Alboher, and Joy Mangano, we've seen how aligning personal passions with professional aspirations can lead to immensely fulfilling and financially rewarding careers, even as add-on or encore careers.

Let's conclude by reflecting on the key insights gained and considering your next steps toward carving your own path to entrepreneurial success.

The first step in building your encore career is simple: reflect on what brings you joy and purpose.

From there, with the plethora of digital tools and platforms available today, the possibilities are endless.

Embrace your passions, skills, and experience, and explore the opportunities they offer. By taking bold action on your ideas, you'll step into a future where your passions pave the way for both personal and professional fulfillment.

Your potential is limitless.

CHAPTER 2

DISCOVERING YOUR PASSION

INTRODUCTION: THE POWER OF PASSION-DRIVEN ENTREPRENEURSHIP

Have you ever imagined turning something you love into a thriving business?

While it might seem daunting, especially later in life, these inspiring stories reveal just how achievable—and rewarding—it can be.

Consider Arianna Huffington, the visionary behind The Huffington Post. Her journey into digital entrepreneurship began later in life, long after she had established herself as an accomplished author and commentator.

When many might have considered slowing down, Arianna saw an opportunity to create a platform blending blog-style content with traditional news.

She faced challenges head-on, navigating the world of online media, and turned those hurdles into stepping stones for what became a groundbreaking online news platform.

Now, think about Colonel Harland Sanders. While his name is synonymous with KFC, his entrepreneurial journey didn't truly begin until after he turned 60?

Sanders had already been through a slew of jobs when he began cooking for people passing by his service station.

Despite setbacks, including the closure of his restaurant, Sanders refused to quit. Instead, he leaned into his exceptional chicken recipe, traveling across the country to find supporters for his vision.

These stories are more than tales of success; they are living proof that passion can spark opportunities at any stage of life. As you reflect on these narratives, consider how your own passions might fuel a new entrepreneurial journey.

CASE STUDY - ARIANNA HUFFINGTON

Arianna Huffington's journey into digital media might seem like it was destined to succeed, but let's not forget the skepticism and self-doubt she faced.

As a seasoned writer and commentator, the digital landscape was unfamiliar territory. Yet, there was something driving her—a persistent vision of creating a space that bridged the gap between personal blogging and professional news.

With the odds stacked high and a firm belief in her idea, Arianna tackled each challenge with a mix of resolve and adaptability.

She had to cultivate a new skill set to navigate digital SEO and media strategies, which wasn't an overnight success.

With determination, she secured financial backing, bringing on board influential voices and talented writers who resonated with her vision.

The result? The Huffington Post didn't just emerge as a player in the media field; it became a pioneer, eventually catching the eye of AOL for a groundbreaking acquisition deal.

Arianna's journey is a testament to the fact that it's not just about starting fresh, but about channeling what you already know and love into new realms.

Her story reassures us all that it's never too late to leap into the unknown and shape a fulfilling career along the way.

CASE STUDY - COLONEL SANDERS

If ever there was a story about perseverance, it's that of Colonel Sanders.

The truth is, "retire" just wasn't part of his vocabulary.

In his 60s, instead of slowing down, Sanders hit the road, recipe in hand, ready to introduce people to the art of perfectly fried chicken.

Each "no" he encountered was just a step closer to "yes."

Sanders' emotional resilience was nothing short of incredible. There were moments of doubt—you bet—but his belief in the potential of his chicken outshone them.

He literally drove from town to town, cooking meals in exchange for the hopes of landing franchise deals. And did it pay off? Absolutely.

By the time he sold his Kentucky Fried Chicken business, his vision had grown into a global fast-food phenomenon.

Sanders' adventure teaches us not just about resilience, but how sticking to what you truly love can turn dreams into an empire—even when the world says it's too late.

As we draw inspiration from the remarkable journeys of Arianna Huffington and Colonel Sanders, it's clear that pursuing our own passions can lead to extraordinary success, no matter when we start.

But you might be wondering, how do you find that driving force within your own life?

Luckily, discovering your passion doesn't have to remain a mystery. With some simple self-reflection techniques, you can uncover what truly excites you and start imagining how those passions might transform into your own entrepreneurial adventure.

Let's dive into practical ways you can explore and identify these passions, paving the way for your own, unique journey, and start building them into your side hustle business.

TECHNIQUES FOR SELF-REFLECTION

Discovering what truly fuels your passion is an exciting yet challenging journey. These self-reflection techniques can help you uncover what genuinely energizes and inspires you.

Passion Inventory

Think of this exercise as a brainstorming session guided by your heart. Reflect on activities that make you lose track of time, and write down everything that comes to mind. For example, if you enjoy transforming empty spaces into lush green sanctuaries, gardening could be a passion worth exploring.

REFLECTION QUESTION:

What moments make you feel most alive and fulfilled?

Why?

Journaling

Start by journaling about moments when you felt most alive. Was it while teaching a friend to cook? Such reflections could spark ideas, like launching online cooking classes. If you love the art of cooking, journaling may reveal your calling: sharing your culinary skills with beginners.

Reflection Question: What recurring activities or experiences come to mind as you reflect in your journal?

Mood Boards

Mood boards are visual tools that help your creativity flow. Collect images, words, and symbols that resonate with your aspirations. This process can help you connect the dots in unexpected ways. For instance, creating a mood board might uncover a passion for interior design, leading to a consulting business.

REFLECTION QUESTION:

What themes or ideas stand out on your mood board?

How might they connect to your interests?

Peer Feedback

Friends and family often see our strengths more clearly than we do. Ask them about the talents they believe you excel in. Their insights might reveal hidden passions. For instance, others might recognize your storytelling ability long before you consider writing a memoir.

What recurring feedback or compliments have others shared about your talents?

REFLECTION QUESTION:

What recurring feedback or compliments do you receive from others about your talents?

By using these tools, the path from discovering your passions to launching a business becomes less intimidating. The journey focuses on building around the activities and interests you love.

While starting something new may feel daunting, remember you're not alone. Many have faced similar fears and successfully turned their dreams into reality—let their stories inspire you.

Once you feel confident aligning your passions with potential business ideas, it's time to solidify those ideas with data-driven insights.

In the next section, we'll explore how to effectively research and analyze the market to ensure your passion project is not only a personal joy but also a professional success.

MARKET RESEARCH AND ANALYSIS

Understanding your passion is just the first step.

How can you transform that passion into something people truly need?

The magic lies in the intersection of your passion and market demand.

This is where market research becomes essential—but don't worry, it's simpler than you might think.

Tools like Google Trends and social media insights can reveal what's trending and how your passions align with current interests.

A great example of effective market research was carried out by Gary Vaynerchuk.

By analyzing online conversations, Gary identified trends and used these insights to help businesses thrive.

He founded VaynerMedia by focusing on what was trending and what resonated with audiences.

Through digital tools, he uncovered what captured people's attention and crafted marketing strategies that aligned with their interests.

To get started, try Google Trends—a tool that acts like a thermometer for current trends.

Enter keywords related to your passion and explore whether interest in these topics is growing.

It might even point you toward the next big opportunity.

Social media is a goldmine for understanding audience preferences.

Observe which posts receive the most engagement—likes, comments, and shares.

These interactions provide valuable insights into what resonates with your audience.

Engage directly with your potential customers through conversations or surveys.

For example, if you're exploring wellness coaching, consider offering free sessions to gather feedback and identify what resonates most.

Remember, it's not just about having the tools, but being curious and open to feedback.

These insights are your guide to where your passion meets demand.

As we move forward, let's think about how to take this well-thought-out passion and market understanding and turn it into a reliable business plan. Not just a project, but a business that could really take off and shape your future.

We'll explore how to make those insights pay off in the real world, by discovering business opportunities.

DISCOVERING BUSINESS OPPORTUNITIES WITH CHATGPT

Once you've clarified your passions, the next step is exploring how to turn them into viable opportunities. Tools like ChatGPT, whether used on its own or as part of platforms like Rubi AI, make this process straightforward. Here's how a gardener might use this tool:

1. Input Your Passion into ChatGPT:

"I have a passion for gardening."

2. Ask ChatGPT to provide some business opportunities related to your passion.

   "Please provide 10 online job opportunities related to gardening."

3. Analyze Trends in the gardening niche:

   "Please research any recent trends for businesses related to gardening."

ChatGPT shows a rise in demand for eco-friendly gardening solutions:

Ask ChatGPT to provide a list of 10 online business opportunities within the eco-friendly gardening niche.

A compelling real-life example is Jackson Greathouse Fall, a brand designer and writer who used ChatGPT to quickly create a thriving side hustle, Green Gadget Guru.

Driven by an innovative mindset, Jackson explored opportunities in the 'sustainable living' niche.

With minimal investment and a single day to launch, he leveraged ChatGPT to brainstorm and refine his business concepts.

Jackson documented his journey on Twitter, where he shared how ChatGPT helped him outline business concepts, suggest eco-friendly products, and generate marketing strategies tailored to sustainability-minded consumers.

Utilizing these insights, he quickly set up Green Gadget Guru, which focuses on providing sustainable living products and actionable tips for eco-conscious living.

His successful endeavor illustrates how digital tools like ChatGPT can empower entrepreneurs to swiftly translate their visions into reality, all while maintaining a focus on sustainability and innovation, while translating a passion into a successful financial outcome.

TRANSLATING PASSION INTO FINANCIAL OUTCOME

Transforming your passion into a profitable business is like perfecting a recipe—it requires the right ingredients and a method tailored to your vision.

Let's break down the process into manageable steps, focusing on storytelling, creating value, and using social media.

Brand Storytelling

Your brand story is the essence of your business—a unique narrative that distinguishes you and forges a connection with your audience.

To craft a compelling brand story, focus on a few key steps:

Start with Your Why:

1. Define the driving force—your "Why"— behind your business.

2. What inspired you to pursue this passion beyond financial gain?

3. Sharing your story can forge an emotional connection with your audience.

Highlight Your Values:

4. Clarify what your business represents—sustainability, innovation, exceptional quality, or another core principle.

5. These values form the backbone of your story and reinforce your dedication to your mission.

Showcase Your Journey:

6. Invite your audience to explore the growth and evolution of your business.

7. Share the challenges you've faced and how you've overcome them, adding authenticity and relatability to your story.

Engage with Your Audience:

8. Make your audience an integral part of your story.

9. Encourage feedback and interaction, showcasing how their input shapes your business.

10. This approach fosters a sense of community around your brand.

By focusing on these steps, you create a brand story that not only tells but engages your audience, turning your business into more than just a product or service—it becomes an experience your customers can relate to.

Crafting Value Propositions

What sets your offering apart? This is where your unique value proposition (UVP) comes into play.

For instance, in a soap business example, a UVP might emphasize the use of organic ingredients, promising purity that mainstream brands cannot match.

Ensure your UVP resonates with your audience's core values—whether it's quality, ethics, or an unparalleled experience.

Leveraging Social Media

Social media serves as today's dynamic marketplace. Platforms like Instagram and TikTok excel at showcasing your creations and fostering connections with potential customers.

Share behind-the-scenes looks at your production process, along with customer testimonials, to build trust and excitement.

Leverage Instagram's shopping features to simplify purchasing, creating a seamless experience for your followers.

STEPS TO CREATE YOUR OWN BUSINESS STRATEGIES

1. Identify Your Core Story: Take time to reflect on the driving force behind your passion and its connection to your product or service. Jot down the key moments and motivations that shape your journey.

2. Define Your Value Proposition: Clearly define what sets your offering apart from what's already on the market. Focus on how it addresses a problem or fulfills a specific need for your audience.

3. Plan Social Media Content: Create a content calendar that includes product showcases, engaging narratives, and interactions with customers. Regularly review analytics to identify the content that resonates most, and refine your strategy accordingly.

4. Engage and Iterate: Leverage feedback from social media followers and customers to enhance your product and strategy. Stay adaptable and responsive to ensure sustained growth.

By sharing your authentic story, defining your unique value, and strategically using digital platforms, you can turn your passion into a thriving business.

Conclusion: Embracing Passion and Turning It Into Action

Reflecting on how passions can be transformed into real-world business opportunities, it's clear that age is not a limitation but a wealth of experience waiting to be tapped.

Consider Arianna Huffington's foray into digital media in her 50s to Colonel Sanders building a global empire in his 60s—both are proof that passion drives perseverance, leading to extraordinary results.

These examples remind us that it's never too late to embark on a new journey or to launch a business that aligns with your deepest passions.

This journey illustrates how discovering your passion, practicing self-reflection, and conducting market research can come together to create a clear roadmap for launching a successful side hustle.

Each aspect plays a critical role—uncovering what truly excites you, understanding yourself deeper, and aligning your passion with market needs—to guide you toward creating a fulfilling and successful business.

So, here's your call to action:

1. Take the first step—start small and approach each step of your journey with enthusiasm and determination.

2. Let your passion guide you toward building something truly meaningful.

As you move from inspiration to implementation, the next chapter will serve as your guide to establishing the operational and legal foundation for your business.

This groundwork will ensure your passion doesn't just remain a dream, but thrives within a robust framework.

Get ready to turn your newfound inspiration into structured, actionable plans that will support your venture's growth and success.

CHAPTER 3

BUILDING THE FOUNDATION OF YOUR BUSINESS

INTRODUCTION: THE IMPORTANCE OF A STRONG FOUNDATION

When Ray Kroc discovered the McDonald brothers' innovative fast-food restaurant in San Bernardino, California, he saw more than just a thriving eatery.

Ray saw an opportunity to take a business with a strong foundation and build something monumental out of it.

At 52 years old, when many might consider winding down, Kroc embarked on the adventure of a lifetime. He envisioned a national franchise that offered not just good food, but also a promise of quality and speed, transforming a small family business into what would become a global icon.

Kroc's journey wasn't without obstacles. Imagine the leap from selling milkshake machines to structuring a burgeoning franchise system—each step required careful planning and a strong foundational business structure.

His success hinged on laying down a robust framework of clear operational guidelines and an unwavering brand identity that could be replicated anywhere. This approach didn't just support growth; it fueled an empire that continues to thrive.

In this chapter, we'll explore how you can build a strong foundation for your business, much like Ray Kroc did when transforming McDonald's into a global empire.

Whether your aim is to scale your passion project or ensure your venture's long-term success, building a sturdy structure is vital.

From understanding the right legal structures to connect with your audience through branding, and effectively planning your finances, each element plays a crucial role in supporting and sustaining your entrepreneurial journey.

Understanding the basics of business legality forms the cornerstone of lasting success.

Just as Kroc realized the importance of legal frameworks in structuring McDonald's, understanding and implementing the right legal business basics is pivotal for any new venture aiming for sustainability and scalability.

UNDERSTANDING LEGAL BUSINESS BASICS

Selecting the right legal structure is a critical step in establishing a strong foundation for your business. Let's break down the main options, just like Ray Kroc had to consider when transforming McDonald's into a franchise giant.

Let's breakdown the common business structures simply:

Sole Proprietorship:

- Definition: A sole proprietorship is the simplest and most common business structure owned and operated by a single individual.

- Pros: Easy to set up, complete control over decisions, straightforward tax process.

- Cons: Personal liability for all debts, harder to raise capital.

- Example: Jane, a 60 year-old therapist with a passion for graphic design, starts a freelance business from home. She enjoys complete control but understands she's personally responsible for her business debts.

Partnership

- Definition: A partnership involves two or more individuals who share ownership, responsibilities, and decision-making in a business.

- Pros: Shared responsibility and resources, complementary skills from partners.

- Cons: Joint liability with partners, potential for disputes between partners.

- Example: Tom and Jerry, skilled in arts and crafts, partner to open a handcrafted gift shop, combining their talents and resources.

Limited Liability Company (LLC)

- Definition: An LLC is a versatile business structure combining the liability protection of a corporation with the tax advantages of a partnership.

- Pros: Limited personal liability, flexible tax options, less formalities than corporations.

- Cons: More paperwork than sole proprietorship, state-specific regulations.

- Example: Mary and Frank, seasoned professionals in their 50s, decided to pivot from their long-standing corporate careers to pursue a venture that reflected their passion for culture and community.

- Mary's experience in corporate finance and Frank's expertise in strategic marketing provided a strong foundation for their entrepreneurial journey.

- With a shared vision and complementary skills, they joined forces to establish a city tour business showcasing the rich history and vibrant culture of their beloved city.

By choosing a Limited Liability Company (LLC), they gained limited personal liability and operational flexibility, enabling them to protect their personal assets while adapting their business strategies to meet evolving needs.

The LLC structure allowed them to leverage their corporate experience in a more personal and impactful way while managing the complexities of state-specific business regulations.

Their entrepreneurial transition exemplifies a thoughtful and strategic shift, harnessing years of professional expertise to create a business that reflects their passion and highlights the unique qualities of their city.

Corporation

- Definition: A corporation is a complex business structure that functions as a separate legal entity owned by shareholders. It provides strong liability protection but requires extensive record-keeping and regulatory compliance.

- Pros: Limited liability, potential to raise money by selling stock, perpetual existence.

- Cons: Complex to form, double taxation, stringent regulatory requirements.

- Example: Alice and her team launched a tech startup with plans for rapid growth and external investment. To facilitate fundraising and scaling, they established a corporation.

UNDERSTANDING LEGAL BUSINESS BASICS: A QUICK GUIDE

Legal Structure	Definition	Pros	Cons
Sole Proprietorship	A straightforward and common structure, where one individual owns and manages the business.	Easy to set up, complete control, straightforward tax process	Personal liability for debts, harder to raise capital.
Partnership	Involves two or more individuals sharing ownership and responsibilities.	Shared responsibility and resources, complementary skills from partners.	Joint liability with partners, potential disputes
Limited Liability Company (LLC)	Offers the liability protection of a corporation with the tax benefits of a partnership.	Limited personal liability, flexible tax options, fewer formalities than corporations.	More paperwork than sole proprietorship, state-specific regulations.
Corporation	A separate legal entity owned by shareholders,	Limited liability, potential to raise money by	Challenging to establish, subject to

	providing strong liability protection, but needing extensive compliance.	selling stock, perpetual existence.	double taxation, and requires extensive regulatory compliance.

As your business evolves, your needs may change, prompting a transition to a business structure.

Consider Alex, a skilled professional in her fifties with a lifelong passion for baking.

She spent years delighting family and friends with her unique recipes, treating baking as both an art and a source of joy.

As her creations garnered more admirers, Alex began to envision a side hustle that could transform her beloved hobby into a thriving business venture.

To take her first step into entrepreneurship, Alex opted for a sole proprietorship.

This choice allowed her to test the waters with minimal overhead, maintaining complete control over her burgeoning business while keeping operations lean and flexible.

Her reputation for quality and detail soon attracted a growing clientele, quickly surpassing her initial expectations.

Faced with increasing demand, Alex decided to take her business to the next level by forming a Limited Liability Company (LLC).

This transition not only protected her personal assets but also positioned her to attract more substantial investments for expansion.

By blending her professional acuity with her baking passion, Alex successfully scaled her side hustle into a business that blends her love for creativity with her seasoned business acumen.

As Alex's story shows, this is not just about making the right choice for today, but ensuring your venture can scale and sustain over time, especially considering the laws of the state (or country) you operate in.

To ensure that you're meeting the regulations required for your business, it's vital to consult with legal, business, and financial professionals who can tailor advice to your specific needs.

With your legal foundation in place, it's time to focus on the essence of your business—your brand.

Think of your legal foundation as the sturdy bones of your business, giving you the freedom to flesh out your personality and style that attracts and connects with your audience.

With the heavy lifting of legality out of the way, you can focus on what really makes your venture stand out.

It's like moving from building the structure of your house to making it a homey environment to invite guests. That's what creating a unique brand can do for a business.

Let's explore how you can create a brand that speaks to your audience and builds lasting relationships.

BRANDING: CONNECTING WITH YOUR AUDIENCE

Branding is more than logos and tagline; it represents the emotional and strategic essence of your business.

A powerful brand identity doesn't just tell people what your business does—it tells them who you are and why they should care.

It builds trust, inspires loyalty, and creates an emotional connection with your audience that can turn one-time buyers into lifelong fans.

Research from WiserNotify reveals that 81% of consumers must trust a brand before making a purchase, with many favoring brands they recognize on social media.

Starting a business later in life can feel daunting, especially with worries like, "What if my brand isn't good enough?" or concern about making a splash in a noisy market.

But remember, branding is an ongoing journey. It evolves as you refine your message and connect more deeply with your audience.

Embrace the process to quell fears and seek comfort in knowing that it's okay to iterate and adjust your brand until it truly reflects your unique vision and resonates with your audience.

These steps can transform branding from an intimidating challenge into a rewarding journey of connection and growth. Let's explore how major corporations have successfully approached branding to achieve market success:

The Apple Way: Branding with Emotion and Strategy

Apple's branding exemplifies the perfect blend of emotional appeal and strategic messaging.

Their "Think Different" campaign didn't just sell products; it sold a vision of innovation and creativity.

Each sleek design and intuitive interface underscores Apple's dedication to creating technology that's not only functional but also aesthetically pleasing and user-friendly.

By keeping their messaging consistent across all platforms, they've maintained a reputation for quality and innovation that resonates deeply with customers worldwide.

McDonald's: From Local to Global

Ray Kroc transformed McDonald's from a local eatery into a global empire by emphasizing the brand's core pillars: quality, service, and cleanliness.

These principles were communicated through consistent messaging and strategic use of colors—red and yellow—to evoke excitement and happiness.

By defining and sticking to these brand values, McDonald's created a familiar and trusted experience for millions of customers around the world.

Apple and McDonald's are large corporations. They have many employees who helped them create and develop their brands.

What actionable steps can small business entrepreneurs take to build a distinctive and memorable brand identity?

Crafting Your Unique Brand Identity

To define a compelling brand identity that resonates with your audience, consider these actionable steps:

- Name and Feedback: Choose a business name that reflects your brand's core values and resonates with your audience. Like Ray Kroc sticking with "McDonald's," ensure it feels right to you and resonates with your audience through surveys or focus groups.

- Legal Considerations: Secure your brand by ensuring your business name is available as a domain trademarking both your name and logo.

- Consistency is Key: Develop a brand identity that reflects your core values. Whether it's through your logo, color scheme, or messaging—everything should work together to tell your brand's story.

- Color and Emotion: Colors can speak volumes about your brand. Use them strategically to evoke the emotions you want your customers to feel.

- Voice and Personality: Define your brand's voice. Whether it's playful like M&Ms or professional like IBM, make sure it's consistent across every customer interaction.

- Leverage Resources: Platforms like Fiverr or 99designs can help bring your vision to life with professional design services. Additionally, engaging in brand strategy workshops can refine your approach and provide useful insights.

A strong brand is fundamental to building a sustainable and scalable business.

Quick Exercise:

Reflect on the emotional essence of your business.

What words do you want people to associate with your brand?

Jot down three adjectives that you hope your brand evokes in your audience.

This will serve as a foundation for building a brand identity that resonates genuinely and leaves a lasting impact.

As you establish your brand, remember it plays an ongoing role in connecting with your audience and guiding your business decisions.

After your brand is clearly defined, showcasing your business's personality and style while attracting your ideal audience, the next step is to bring your business brand to life in the online digital world.

An effective online presence is crucial for introducing your brand to a broader audience.

Your branding efforts have laid the groundwork, crafting the story and image you want to share with the world.

Now it's time to extend your brand's reach by creating a compelling online presence through your website and social media platforms—your digital handshake to connect with customers worldwide.

Let's dive into how you can leverage your brand to build an impactful online presence.

BUILDING YOUR ONLINE PRESENCE: A STEP-BY-STEP GUIDE TO SUCCESS

In today's interconnected world, a robust online presence is essential—it serves as your business's first handshake with the digital audience.

Long before the digital age, Ray Kroc recognized the value of visibility and consistency in scaling McDonald's, principles that remain relevant today.

Today, the internet serves as the vital stage where your business can reach its audience globally.

A Forbes report, "Building a Brand: Why A Strong Digital Presence Matters," highlights a Salesforce survey revealing that 85% of consumers research online before making a purchase, with websites serving as the primary resource.

Let's explore a step-by-step guide to establishing your business online with confidence and ease.

Step-by-Step Guide to Creating Your Professional Website

Step 1: Choosing the Perfect Domain Name

Simplicity is Key:

- Think of your domain name as your business's digital address—it should be memorable and relevant to your brand.

- Pick a name that's easy to remember and is relevant to your business. For instance, Mary, who is starting an online home-baked goods store, opts for "MarysBakes.com."

Check Availability:

- Use services like GoDaddy or Namecheap to ensure the domain name you want is available. (A ".com" domain is often considered preferred.)

Pro Tip:

- Secure your domain name early to prevent others from claiming it.

Step 2: Choosing the Right Website Platform

Consider Your Needs:

Are you planning to sell products directly from your website? E-commerce platforms like Shopify make handling transactions seamless and efficient.

User-Friendly Options:

If you're new to website creation, platforms like Wix or Squarespace offer intuitive drag-and-drop interfaces.

Business Tip:

- Just as Ray Krock standardized McDonald's operations for consistency, select a website platform that complements your business's unique needs.

Step 3: Designing an Engaging Website

Template Selection:

- Select a pre-designed template that reflects your brand's aesthetic and values.

- Mary selects a template with warm tones and cozy imagery to match her home-baking brand.

Customization:

- Adjust colors, fonts, and images to align with your brand's identity. Consistency here will build recognition and trust.

Step 4: Creating Compelling Content

Tell Your Story:

- Share what makes your business unique. Mary's "About" page shares how her grandma's cherished recipes inspired her baking business, adding a personal touch that resonates with customers.

Use engaging strategies:

- Use high-quality images and text that will engage your audience.

- Regularly post informative blog articles.

Step 5: Optimizing Your Website for Search Engines (SEO)

- Use tools like Google Keyword Planner to understand what your audience is searching for.

- Identify relevant keywords for your industry and incorporate them naturally into your website's content to enhance search engine visibility.

- Importance: Good SEO practices help your site rank higher in search results, increasing visibility

Step 6: Ensuring Your Website's Security and Longevity

Security First:

- Secure your website with an SSL certificate to protect customer data, especially if you operate an e-commerce site.

Regular Maintenance Updates:

- Keep your site platform and plugins up-to-date to avoid security vulnerabilities.

Leveraging Tools to Conquer Fear and Build Your Business

Starting an online business can feel overwhelming, particularly with the rapid pace of technological advancements like AI.

Fortunately, tools like AutoFunnel.ai simplify the process of building professional websites, automating tasks to empower even the least tech-savvy entrepreneurs to succeed.

Remember, every tech giant began with small steps and overcame their share of challenges along the way.

With the right tools and a growth mindset, your online business dream can become reality.

Your digital storefront is a cornerstone of your business foundation. Consider Ray Kroc's golden arches: they became an enduring symbol of reliability and trust for customers worldwide.

With your brand ready to engage customers online, the next critical step in building a resilient business is effective financial planning

Prudent financial management ensures your business remains stable and ready to seize growth opportunities.

In the next section, we'll explore how to craft a financial plan and strategies to transform your business from a passion project into a profitable enterprise.

Financial Planning: Setting the Stage for Success

To Plan or Not to Plan—That is the Question

Among small online businesses, the necessity of a financial or business plan is often a topic of debate.

Proponents contend that a formal business plan serves as a clear roadmap, aligning future activities with defined objectives while instilling confidence in potential investors.

It outlines strategies, financial projections, and key performance indicators, ensuring that a business is prepared for potential challenges and opportunities.

On the other hand, some entrepreneurs argue that the dynamic nature of online markets makes formal plans obsolete.

Instead, they advocate for an adaptable approach that combines learning and planning through real-time experimentation.

This perspective, rooted in the principles of lean startups, emphasizes agility, problem-solving in real time, and iterative development.

The decision ultimately comes down to the individual entrepreneur's style and the specific needs of their business. Some find peace of mind in having a detailed plan, while others thrive on flexibility and responsiveness.

In either case, having a plan—whether formal or informal—can guide your business to not only survive, but thrive.

Let's break down how to create a financial framework that supports your entrepreneurial journey.

CRAFTING A FLEXIBLE AND EFFECTIVE BUSINESS PLAN

Consider your business plan a flexible roadmap, not a rigid stone tablet.

A detailed business plan can help secure funding and define clear goals, but balancing structure with adaptability is crucial for navigating unforeseen challenges.

Pros:

- Clarity and Direction: A well-thought-out plan helps you understand your market, competition, and financial needs. It sets clear goals and a step-by-step strategy.

- Attracts Investors: A detailed plan can attract investors who want to see a clear path to profitability.

Cons:

- Rigid Structure: Being too rigid can hinder your ability to pivot as market conditions change.

- Time Intensive: Preparing a full business plan can take time you might prefer to spend on immediate business problems.

SETTING FINANCIAL GOALS AND MANAGING CASH FLOW

Maintaining financial health requires setting clear goals and managing cash flow effectively, regardless of whether you choose a formal plan.

Take Amazon, for example: It started as a small operation focused on customer satisfaction, but grew into a global giant through consistent innovation and diligent financial management.

By setting a balance between short-term actions and long-term goals, you can adapt as needed while keeping your business growing.

- Create Short-term and Long-term Goals:
    - Establish achievable short-term milestones that align with your long-term vision. This dual focus keeps you motivated and ensures steady progress toward your goals.

- Understand Cash Flow:

- Keep an eye on your cash inflows and outflows regularly to avoid unexpected financial surprises.

- Track your "burn rate"—the speed at which you're spending funds—and your "runway," which is the time your business can sustain operations with existing resources. These metrics provide valuable insights for making informed financial decisions.

- This will help you make smarter financial decisions and plan for the future more effectively.

EXAMPLE: ELLA'S BOUTIQUE

Ella owns a small online boutique selling handmade crafts. She uses a flexible business plan framework:

- Short-term Goal:

  - Boost website traffic by 20% within three months through targeted social media campaigns.

- Long-term Goal:

  - Introduce a seasonal product line in the next fiscal year to diversify offerings.

- Cash Flow Management:

  - Ella checks her cash position weekly, ensuring she's prepared for upcoming expenses like inventory restocking.

As you implement these financial strategies, remember that a strong business foundation is the bedrock of lasting success.

Just like a well-composed financial outline supports growth and stability, so too do the stories of entrepreneurs who have paved their paths with creativity and foresight.

The key is to plan clearly, act wisely, and adjust as necessary. This approach builds a sustainable path for your venture.

In the next section, we'll explore the inspiring journey of Jim Henson and how he laid the groundwork for a thriving enterprise and built an enduring legacy. His story offers further insights into successful entrepreneurship.

Jim Henson: A Case Study in Laying Strong Business Foundations

Jim Henson, the visionary creator of The Muppets, built an empire by blending creativity, strategic foresight, and relentless innovation.

Henson's journey exemplifies key strategies for success: building a strong brand, connecting with audiences, and forging strategic partnerships.

His visionary approach blended creativity with strategic foresight, demonstrating the power of a well-crafted brand and the significance of engaging storytelling that resonates with audiences globally.

By forging strategic partnerships and staying true to a distinct brand identity, Henson not only captivated viewers but also laid down a robust foundation for lasting success.

His journey serves as an inspiring model for entrepreneurs aiming to establish a strong business foundation by building a brand that's as dynamic and enduring as his beloved puppets.

VISION, INNOVATION, AND LEGACY

Jim Henson envisioned revolutionizing puppetry by seamlessly blending it with innovative storytelling and the medium of television.

Through his relentless pursuit of combining art with entertainment, Henson created groundbreaking works like The Muppets and Sesame Street, which evolved into enduring cultural icons.

Henson's vision transcended traditional entertainment, integrating education and fostering a global impact that secured his enduring legacy.

Entrepreneurs can draw inspiration from Henson's clear vision, which guided his innovations and set the strategic direction for his work, illustrating the power of purpose in driving business success.

STRATEGIC PARTNERSHIPS

Henson formed a pivotal partnership with Joan Ganz Cooney, which resulted in the creation of the educational classic Sesame Street.

This collaboration significantly broadened his audience and amplified the educational value of his creations.

By aligning with partners who shared his vision and values, Henson effectively leveraged complementary strengths and resources to enhance his impact.

EMBRACING TECHNOLOGY

Henson embraced technology early in his career, utilizing advanced techniques to bring greater expression and mobility to his puppets.

His willingness to invest in and experiment with emerging technologies ensured his work remained at the industry's forefront.

For entrepreneurs, embracing innovation is essential for gaining a competitive edge and driving progress in today's dynamic business landscape.

CONSISTENT BRANDING

The Muppets consistently embodied a brand image defined by humor, creativity, and heartfelt connection.

Henson's ability to infuse each character with unique personalities that resonate globally has maintained his brand's instant recognition and endearment.

A consistent brand message fosters customer loyalty and builds enduring emotional connections—an indispensable strategy for long-term business success.

EXPANDING TALENT

Henson recognized the value of cultivating talent and assembling a team aligned with his creative vision.

By fostering an environment that encouraged creativity and collaboration, he ensured the brand's continued evolution and success.

By fostering and empowering talent, Henson ensured that his legacy endured beyond his direct involvement, showcasing the essential role of human capital in building a resilient business foundation.

Jim Henson's story is a testament to how vision, innovation, and collaboration can create a powerful and enduring business foundation.

His approach provides a blueprint for entrepreneurs looking to build not just a brand, but a legacy that endures.

Jim Henson's remarkable journey reminds us of the transformative power of strategic thinking and creativity in building a sustainable, scalable business, and a legacy that endures.

Armed with these insights, we now transition to the final section of this chapter, where we'll distill key lessons and outline the essential steps to advance your entrepreneurial journey.

CONCLUSION: BUILDING DREAMS ON A STRONG FOUNDATION

As this chapter concludes, let's reflect on the essential lessons that form the foundation of entrepreneurial success—especially for seasoned professionals over 50 entering new business ventures.

Starting a new venture can feel daunting, particularly when transitioning from years of professional experience into unchartered territory.

However, building a solid foundation ensures your business is equipped to grow and adapt, leveraging your wealth of experience to navigate new waters.

This chapter explored essential steps, including selecting the right legal structure, creating a memorable brand, building a strong online presence, and managing finances effectively.

For professionals over 50, these steps transcend mere procedural checklists. They serve as a strategic framework that blends your real-world wisdom with emerging opportunities, fostering innovation and resilience.

Embarking on entrepreneurship later in life is undoubtedly a bold step, yet it is within these challenges that immense opportunities lie.

Imagine this: you've built a strong foundation, transforming it into a springboard that propels your lifelong dreams into tangible achievements.

By harnessing your unique expertise and honing in on what distinguishes your business, you're not merely constructing a stable fortress—you're paving the way for dynamic growth and innovation.

Your persistence, combined with your extensive professional insights and experience, will now propel you toward achieving your dreams.

Looking ahead, with a strong foundation beneath you, you are well-positioned to embrace emerging technologies and seize new opportunities.

The journey forward involves harnessing technological tools such as AI and digital platforms, seamlessly integrating them with your existing expertise to enhance operations and broaden your reach.

Embrace these technological advancements to turn potential into performance, propelling your business forward to unprecedented heights and achieving success with the wisdom and confidence that only seasoned experience and insights can provide.

CHAPTER 4

NAVIGATING THE TECH TERRAIN

EMBRACING TECHNOLOGY: FROM INSURANCE BROKER TO DIGITAL INNOVATOR

Across bustling cities and tranquil suburbs, professionals are embracing technology to transform their careers.

Among these trailblazers is David, a former insurance broker whose inspiring journey highlights the power of reinvention.

While he excelled in offering personalized advice and tailored coverage plans, David's curiosity about the digital world drove him to explore uncharted territory.

David's Leap into the Unknown

Soft-spoken and meticulous, David was far from a stereotypical tech enthusiast.

Transitioning from a secure career in insurance to creating bespoke timepieces online presented significant challenges.

Initially, the digital landscape appeared vast and intimidating, filled with complex e-commerce platforms, digital marketing strategies, and AI tools that often seemed more perplexing than promising.

David's early efforts were riddled with challenges, and at times, his aspirations seemed unattainable.

However, every setback became an opportunity to learn, adapt, and innovate.

He reframed his journey as more than a career shit—it was a chance to merge his passion with technology.

Each crafted timepiece was a testament to his relentless spirit and newfound growth using learned digital skills.

A Digital Embrace: David's Triumphs

David's story transcends watches or career changes—it's about wholeheartedly embracing transformation.

By blending his craftmanship with cutting-edge technology, he successfully expanded his reach to international markets.

His journey mirrors the challenges and opportunities many professionals encounter as they transition into the digital age.

Like David, stepping into the tech world may bring challenges. Yet each obstacle offers a gateway to growth.

Drawing from David's experience, let's uncover practical strategies to make technology your most valuable business ally.

Reassurance and Practical Solutions

For many budding entrepreneurs, diving into the world of technology can be daunting.

There's often a fear that you'll lose the personal touch, get caught up in complex technicalities, or just not keep pace with the rapid changes.

But, as David's journey shows us, technology is here to help, not hinder.

Here are a few approachable steps to get started:

Start Small:

- Begin with user-friendly tools to build confidence. For example, Canva's intuitive drag-and-drop features make it ideal for creating professional visuals—from social media graphics to flyers and presentations—with ease.

Learn from Others:

- Draw inspiration from success stories like David's. Many have walked this path before you and have not only navigated the tech landscape but thrived within it.

Embrace the Learning Process:

- Technology is always evolving, offering fresh opportunities for those open to continuous learning.

- Take Squarespace, for example. It's a user-friendly platform perfect for those who want to set up their website without fuss.

You can easily craft a polished site to showcase your products and connect with audiences worldwide.

By taking these small, manageable steps, you'll find yourself gaining confidence and skill in incorporating technology into your business.

Just like David, starting with the basics can lead to remarkable transformations and new opportunities.

As we move forward, let's explore some fundamental technologies and their roles in modern business.

Understanding these tools can empower you to take control of your own transformation, just as David did.

Use these tools as stepping stones to embark on your journey of innovation and growth.

SIMPLIFYING ARTIFICIAL INTELLIGENCE (AI) BASICS

Artificial Intelligence might once have seemed like a concept out of science fiction, but today, it's a practical and indispensable tool for many small business owners.

- Artificial Intelligence: AI, a branch of computer science, focuses on developing systems that perform tasks traditionally requiring human intelligence, like recognizing patterns, making decisions, and understanding natural language.

- Chatbots: Automated programs designed to interact with customers via text or voice. These virtual assistants efficiently handle routine inquiries, book appointments, and even complete transactions, allowing you to concentrate on more critical aspects of your business.

- Large Language Models (LLMs): This refers to advanced AI systems, trained on vast amounts of text data to understand and generate human-like text. Examples include OpenAI's ChatGPT and Google's Gemini (formerly Bard), which are capable of translating languages, summarizing text, and answering questions based on context.

- Prompts: The inputs or instructions you give to an AI system to elicit a response or action. Think of them as the questions or commands that guide the AI to perform a task or provide information relevant to your needs.

- Prompt Engineering: Think of prompt engineering as the skill of creating a question or request (AKA: the Prompt) that you will post to the AI chatbot. The goal is to craft prompts that elicit the most accurate and helpful responses.

- It's all about being clear and specific with your queries to ensure the AI provides exactly what you need. Just like in a good conversation, the more precise you are, the better the response you'll get.

So how can these tools help a small business entrepreneur?

Imagine you're an artisan bakery owner, juggling emails, customer inquiries, and orders all day long.

Now, imagine you have chatbots, LLMs like ChatGPT and Gemini, and platforms that include multiple AI tools, like

Rubi AI (with its multiple LLMs, and tools for image, video, and music creation).

You now have the capacity to more easily and quickly handle those everyday tasks.

These technologies seamlessly answer questions, process orders, and provide tailored recommendations based on customer preferences. They can work tirelessly 24/7, allowing you to focus on what you love most—baking!

However, it's important to note that it's important to personalize what AI creates for you, and check for accuracy, since they are not you and might not have the most accurate information.

Let's look at another example, discovering how AI can help a small business owner, like Sam, a fictional example of a small business owner who runs a cozy bookstore.

Sam was overwhelmed with customer queries and managing social media engagement.

When Sam integrated a chatbot on his website, it transformed his business operations. The bot answered frequently asked questions, provided personalized book recommendations, and collected customer feedback.

This improved customer satisfaction and freed up Sam's time to organize events and book readings, ultimately increasing sales and fostering stronger community engagement.

As you can see, embracing AI tools doesn't mean losing the personal touch;. Instead, it can amplify it by providing a seamless and engaging customer experience.

In addition, by getting a handle on the basics of AI, you're setting yourself up to tap into its more sophisticated tools, which are key for boosting your business's productivity and expansion.

With these essentials under your belt, you're ready to start utilizing AI solutions that streamline operations and accelerate growth.

These technologies serve as powerful assistants, enabling you to grow and manage your business with greater efficiency and confidence.

Exploring AI Tools

AI technology extends beyond just chatbots. It offers diverse solutions that enhance various facets of business operations:

AI Generated Personas:

AI-generated personas are detailed customer profiles that represent your target audience, created using artificial intelligence.

These personas can be used to help businesses tailor their marketing and product development efforts, based on the demographics and buying patterns of your target audience.

For example, by using AI to understand the ideal customer persona for a boutique, you can customize promotions and inventory planning based on predicted purchasing behaviors.

AI Image Generation:

AI platforms such as DALL-E or Midjourney transform text descriptions into compelling visuals.

If you're running a boutique, imagine designing eye-catching marketing posters or product visuals with AI-generated art, all without needing a graphic designer.

AI Video Generation:

Tools such as Synthesia, Pictory, and now Sora from Open AI, simplify the creation of engaging video content from scripts.

For a small business, this means you can produce professional promotional videos or product demos to boost your online presence and engagement, even if you lack videography expertise.

AI Music Generation:

With platforms like Amper Music, Jukedeck, and Rubi Music, you can craft unique soundtracks that enhance your promotional materials.

Consider an online ad that's complemented by AI-composed music, delivering a brand experience that resonates more deeply with your audience.

Comprehensive AI Platforms:

Platforms such as Rubi AI and You.com offer all-in-one AI solutions.

They bundle together various AI tools to really streamline how your business runs, like creating business plans, ai-generate images, music, and videos, or creating copy for emails, ads, and more.

Whether you're looking to sharpen up your operations or boost how you engage with customers, these platforms offer resources that naturally fit into your existing business setup. They're a smart choice for small ventures focused on becoming more efficient and innovative.

Each of these AI tools offers a unique opportunity to elevate your business, turning technological advancements into practical, impactful applications.

These examples only scratch the surface, and new tools are introduced daily.

However, the introduction of new tools, particularly those leveraging advanced technology, often sparks fear of the unknown, potentially hindering progress toward our goals.

It's entirely normal to feel apprehensive about diving into the unknown. But these days, overcoming these tech-related anxieties is often crucial for building a business that's not only sustainable but also scalable.

Many successful entrepreneurs once stood where you are now—at the starting line of their tech journey. By embracing technology, they unlocked opportunities for remarkable success.

Meet Jane, a 52-year-old entrepreneur who owned a charming clothing boutique in a small town.

Taking her store online felt intimidating, like stepping into a foreign territory with unfamiliar rules.

Her biggest hurdles were figuring out how to showcase her unique inventory digitally and managing online customer interactions.

But, by starting small with manageable e-commerce tools like Shopify, she slowly got the hang of things.

Sure, there were bumps along the way, like learning to optimize her product images for faster load times and dealing with occasional delivery mishaps.

Yet, with each challenge, she gained valuable insights, broadening her customer reach and boosting sales by a remarkable 40% in her first year online.

Another example is Tom, a talented self-employed graphic designer now in his early 60's, who was used to creating art with traditional methods.

The thought of using AI-based design software was daunting; he feared it might erode the personal touch that defined his work.

His challenges included navigating the initial setup of these tools and overcoming his skepticism about whether AI could genuinely match his creative flair.

However, after seeing peers succeed, he gave it a try.

Initially, the software felt clunky. But as he began to see how AI could handle time-consuming tasks, within months, Tom discovered new ways to blend his artistic skills with tech innovations.

This allowed him to offer more comprehensive services, tapping into a wider market and significantly growing his client base and income.

Both Jane and Tom started their e-commerce adventures with hesitations.

Yet, by embracing the learning process and leveraging technology, they turned potential roadblocks into opportunities for success.

Just like them, by stepping beyond initial fears, you can discover how integrating the right tools can revolutionize your business.

Do you have any fears about incorporating technology into your new business startup?

Here are some practical strategies to help you overcome common tech fears and confidently integrate technology into your business.

Actionable Advice for Overcoming Tech Fears

- Start with Small Steps: Begin by integrating one simple tech tool into your daily routine. As you get comfortable, gradually introduce more advanced tools.

- Continuous Learning: Enroll in short online courses or tutorials related to the technologies you're interested in. Platforms like Coursera or Udemy offer courses that cater to beginners.

- Peer Support: Connect with other entrepreneurs who have successfully navigated similar challenges.

Joining forums or local business groups can pro-vide you with valuable insights and encourage-ment.

- Focus on Benefits: Clearly define what you want to achieve by adopting new technology. Keeping your end goals in mind can help maintain your motiva-tion and reduce anxiety.

Overcoming tech fears is a journey, just like any other as-pect of entrepreneurship. By taking initiative, seeking sup-port, and gradually adapting to new tools, you can position your business for long-term success and sustainability.

Reflection Exercise:

Before we continue, take a moment to reflect on how AI could transform your new business.

Think about one task that takes up a lot of your time or feels repetitive—perhaps it's handling customer inquiries, scheduling meetings, or even managing inventory.

Consider how an AI tool could take over this task, freeing you to focus on more strategic, creative aspects of your business.

Jot down your thoughts and envision the impact this change could have.

This exercise is all about recognizing AI as an ally, ready to take some weight off your shoulders.

Now that you've started thinking about AI's potential to streamline your operations, it's time to explore another key facet of digital business: e-commerce.

Just as AI can enhance efficiency and free you up for more creative tasks, e-commerce offers a platform to expand your reach and connect with customers in new ways.

Let's delve into how you can leverage e-commerce to grow your business, tapping into the digital marketplace to transcend physical boundaries and engage a global audience.

E-COMMERCE ESSENTIALS

Mastering e-commerce is essential for any modern business aiming to thrive in today's digital marketplace. But what exactly is e-commerce, and how can you use it to grow your business?

E-commerce, short for electronic commerce, involves buying and selling of goods or services online.

It includes activities like online shopping, digital payments, internet banking, and ticket booking.

E-commerce allows businesses to reach a global audience, offering products and services through digital platforms without the limitations of physical location.

Here's a streamlined approach focusing on three key areas to help you build an effective online store.

1. Selecting the Right Platform

Selecting the right platform is an important decision to make when planning your e-commerce strategy.

Platforms like Etsy, Sam Cart, Shopify, Stan Store, and WooCommerce, each offer unique advantages tailored to different business needs:

- Etsy: Perfect for artisans and crafters, Etsy specializes in selling handmade, vintage, or uniquely manufactured items. If your business focuses on creative custom goods, Etsy provides the advantage of an established community eager for niche products.

- Sam Cart: This platform is designed for those who need a straightforward way to sell individual products or services. With features focused on conversion optimization, including upsell and order bump capabilities, Sam Cart is great for businesses looking to maximize sales on single product offers.

- Shopify: Known for its intuitive interface, Shopify is perfect for businesses wanting an all-encompassing solution. Its customizable templates and comprehensive app ecosystem cater to those who prefer easy store setup and management without needing in-depth technical know-how.

- Stan Store: Tailored for creators and influencers, Stan Store allows seamless e-commerce integration with content creation. It enables businesses to manage sales directly from social media profiles, making it ideal for those whose sales strategies heavily rely on social platforms.

- WooCommerce: As a plugin for WordPress, WooCommerce offers extensive customization for businesses already using WordPress. It provides flexibility and diverse customization options, ideal for creating a highly personalized shopping experience.

2. Managing Payments

A secure and efficient payment system is critical for building customer trust and ensuring smooth transactions:

- Use services like PayPal, Stripe, or Square for reliable and secure payment processing.

- Make sure your payment options are diverse enough to cater to international customers, including credit/debit cards, digital wallets, and even cryptocurrency if applicable.

- Integrate SSL certificates to encrypt transactions and protect sensitive customer data.

3. Enhancing Customer Engagement

Creating an engaging shopping experience encourages customer loyalty and repeat business:

- Leverage email marketing tools to engage customers with newsletters, tailored promotions, and cart recovery reminders.

- Implement live chat support and chatbots to provide immediate assistance and enhance customer service.

- Create a loyalty program offering points or discounts to encourage repeat purchases.

These e-commerce essentials help lay a strong foundation for online success.

As you build your platform, remember to continuously adapt to new trends and customer needs.

With the right technology and strategy in place, your business can scale and sustain growth effectively.

After launching your e-commerce store, prioritizing digital security is essential to protect your business and customers.

The digital marketplace offers immense opportunities, but it also comes with the need to protect your customer's sensitive information.

That's where cybersecurity steps in—it's all about locking down your business's data to build trust and resilience.

Let's explore the key practices to shield your enterprise from cyber threats and ensure a secure online presence.

CYBERSECURITY 101: PROTECTING YOUR DIGITAL ASSETS

In today's digital world, protecting your business from cyber threats is just as essential as making a profit.

Cybersecurity can seem daunting for beginners, but it's crucial to protect your growing business.

Breaking down the steps can make it manageable and reassuring. But first, let's tackle some definitions:

HTTP (Hypertext Transfer Protocol) is the basic language of the web, enabling your browser and servers to communicate and transfer data. It operates in plain text, so it can be read easily by anyone who gains access to it. Thus, having a URL with an "HTTP" address is not preferred due to lack of security guardrails.

HTTPS (Hypertext Transfer Protocol Secure) is an advanced version of HTTP that encrypts data that's transferred between the web server and the browser, offering greater security. It's like an upgraded version with a security guard, so that web chats are private, ensuring that your data stays safe from prying eyes.

SSL (Secure Sockets Layer) Certification upgrades an HTTP connection to the more secure HTTPS version. So what are SSL Certificates?

SSL Certificates

An SSL certificate is essentially a digital handshake that secures your online interactions by encrypting data.

SSL stands for Secure Sockets Layer, and the certificate is a small data file installed on a web server that provides extra security for your web address. It's what provides the "HTTPS" in your web address.

When customers visit your site, they look for that padlock icon and the "HTTPS" in your web address—it's a sign that their personal details, like credit card information, are safe from prying eyes.

Why should it be important?

Having an SSL certificate is essential for building customer trust.

It tells them that your site is secure, protecting their data from potential cyber threats.

Additionally, SSL boosts your site's credibility—not only with customers, but also with search engines like Google, which favor HTTPS sites in rankings.

In short, think of SSL Certificates as your online security badge.

They're not just about safety; they're an integral part of gaining customer trust and enhancing your business's reputation in the digital landscape.

While your SSL certificate provides frontline defense for your website, enhancing security doesn't stop there.

Just as securing your website is vital, protecting the keys to your business—your passwords—is equally important.

Creating strong passwords is another essential step in safeguarding your business's digital assets.

Let's dive into how you can craft robust, effective passwords that complement your overall cybersecurity strategy.

Creating Strong Passwords

1. Use Long Passphrases: Create a passphrase by combining unrelated words, making it long and hard to guess.

2. Include Symbols, Numbers, and Upper/Lowercase Letters: A combination of these elements makes passwords harder to crack.

3. Avoid Using Personal Information: Never use birthdays, names, or easily accessible personal details.

4. Change Passwords Regularly: Update passwords every three months and use a password manager to keep them secure.

Implementing robust cybersecurity measures, like SSL certificates and strong passwords, sets the groundwork for safeguarding your business.

These proactive steps ensure that your enterprise is resilient against cyber threats.

Let's consider a real-world example with Maria's Online Boutique, illustrating how such security protocols can make all the difference in protecting customer data and maintaining trust in the face of digital challenges.

Case Study: Maria's Online Boutique

Maria, the owner of a small online boutique, experienced a cyberattack that targeted her customers' data.

Thanks to SSL certificates and strong password protocols, Maria quickly restricted access, protecting her customers' trust and securing her business.

This swift action not only protected her assets but reinforced her dedication to customer security.

After Maria's swift action in securing her boutique, the next logical step is leveraging social media to grow her business.

Secure foundations allow businesses to confidently engage with larger audiences.

Let's explore how you can use social media to confidently reach a broader audience and effectively enhance your business growth.

LEVERAGING SOCIAL MEDIA

In today's digital age, platforms like Facebook, Instagram, LikedIn, TikTok, and YouTube offer powerful tools for connecting with potential customers and growing your business.

Here's a strategic way to get started with your Social Media presence.

Step-by-Step Guide to Creating a Social Media Strategy

1. Identify Your Goals: Start by defining what you want to achieve through social media. Whether it's increasing brand awareness, generating leads, or boosting sales, having clear objectives will guide your strategy.

2. Know Your Audience: Research and understand who your target audience is. Get to know their demographics, interests, and online behavior. Tailor your content in a way that resonates with them.

3. Choose the Right Platforms:

   - Facebook: Perfect for reaching a wide audience with diverse content. Use articles, videos, and live events to engage your community and drive interaction.

   - Instagram: Best for visually-driven content. Share high-quality images, engaging stories, and reels to capture your audience's attention.

   - LinkedIn: Best for B2B marketing and professional networking. Share industry insights, company updates, and thought-leadership articles to build your professional presence.

- TikTok: Perfect for creative, short-form video content. Capture attention with trends, challenges, and authentic storytelling that resonates with a younger, dynamic audience.

- It is increasingly used for business content, with short-form videos, TikTok Shop, and live events.

- YouTube: Great for longer video content. Create tutorials, product demos, and vlogs to provide value and establish authority in your field.

4. Content Creation:

- Create a content calendar to ensure consistency across platforms.

- Create a mix of content types: educational posts, behind-the-scenes glimpses, customer testimonials, and interactive content like polls or Q&As to keep the audience engaged.

5. Engage with Your Audience: Respond promptly to comments and messages to build relationships and foster a loyal community.

6. Analyze and Adjust: Use analytics tools to track performance and determine what's working. Adjust your strategy based on these insights to optimize engagement and reach.

Example in Action

Consider a small cafe using Instagram to showcase daily specials, collaborate with local influencers, and build a loyal online community through consistent, authentic content.

On LinkedIn, the café shares posts about sustainable sourcing and industry trends, reaching a broader professional audience.

As you build your social media presence, remember that these platforms are more than just tools; they're essential for building a community around your brand.

With a solid social media strategy in place, you're poised to drive traffic and boost engagement.

Now, it's time to integrate these efforts with robust e-commerce tools that will cement your business's online presence and streamline sales.

Let's explore the e-commerce essentials needed to convert these interactions into tangible results.

FUTURE-PROOFING YOUR BUSINESS

In today's fast-paced technological landscape, staying ahead and keeping your business relevant requires forward-thinking strategies.

Future-proofing your business isn't just about surviving the latest trends; it's about anticipating changes and using them to drive growth.

Here's a guide to help you keep your business at the forefront of innovation:

Staying Updated on Tech Trends

Continuous Learning:

1. Make it a habit to read industry reports, attend webinars, and participate in forums related to your field.

2. Being well-informed about the latest technologies will help you make strategic decisions.

Networking:

3. Network with industry peers and experts through conferences and events.

4. This not only offers insights into new trends but also potential collaborations that can drive innovation.

Tech News Subscriptions:

5. Subscribe to reputable tech news websites and newsletters.

6. Platforms like TechCrunch, Wired, and GeekWire offer valuable insights into emerging trends and technological advancements.

Emerging Technologies

Blockchain:

1. Often associated with cryptocurrencies, blockchain technology has far more to offer. However, the technology has much more to offer.

2. Think of blockchain as a super-secure digital ledger—a virtual notebook.

3. Blockchain permanently records every transaction and verifies it across a network of computers, making it easier to track products and ensure quality.

4. It's designed to be nearly impossible to alter, providing transparency and security.

For small businesses, blockchain offers opportunities to create smart contracts and improve supply chain transparency.

This technology is all about bringing trust and efficiency to your business dealings.

It enables you to operate with confidence and clarity, ensuring transactions are traceable and reliable while significantly reducing fraud risk.

Internet of Things (IoT):

1. IInternet of Things (IoT) refers to a network of devices that connect to the internet to exchange information.

2. These devices—ranging from home gadgets and wearable fitness trackers to factory machines—gather and provide real-time data.

3. That information can enhance a business's operations, make processes smoother, offer energy-efficient smart appliances, and improve decision-making by offering up-to-the-minute information.

4. For small businesses, think of IoT as a digital assistant that monitors operations in real time, improving efficiency.

5. These innovations automate daily tasks, paving the way for automation through Artificial Intelligence.

6. Artificial Intelligence and Automation:

7. AI can streamline operations, from customer service chatbots to automated inventory management.

8. These technologies free up resources, enabling business owners to focus on strategic growth.

Practical Steps to Future-Proof

Adopt Flexible Technologies:

1. Select technology solutions that are both adaptable and scalable.

2. Cloud-based services, for example, allow you to scale your usage and resources as your business grows.

Invest in Staff Training:

3. Ensure your team has the skills necessary to effectively handle new technologies.

4. Regular training sessions ensure that everyone stays aligned and is prepared to embrace change.

5. Pilot Emerging Tech:

6. Launch pilot projects to test emerging technology.

7. This is a low-risk way to evaluate how a new tool or system performs within your business context.

By staying attuned to technological advancements and remaining adaptable, your business can not only weather the change but also thrive amidst it.

Reflecting on the technological landscape we've navigated, it's clear that staying informed and adaptable is your business's greatest asset.

Now, let's wrap up our journey with a focus on how all these elements come together in navigating the digital landscape to propel your business forward."

CASE-STUDY: Mark - Sales Executive Turned Tech-Savvy Digital Marketer

Meet Mark, a seasoned sales executive with over 30 years of experience in traditional advertising.

At 55, Mark could have easily remained in his comfort zone, but he chose to pivot and explore digital marketing—a move that many considered daunting for someone his age.

Mark started by immersing himself in online courses to learn the latest marketing strategies.

He began experimenting with social media campaigns while harnessing the power of SEO and content marketing.

A turning point for Mark came when he leveraged AI-driven analytics tools to refine his marketing approach, allowing him to connect more effectively with a broader audience.

Within a year, Mark turned his newfound knowledge into a consulting business, helping other companies elevate their digital strategies.

His clients were not only impressed by his expertise, but also inspired by his ability to adapt and embrace new technologies.

Today, Mark's business thrives, serving as a model for what's possible when experience is blended with technology.

CONCLUSION: NAVIGATING THE DIGITAL LANDSCAPE

As we conclude this chapter, the journeys of David and Mark illustrate what's possible when you embrace technology with an open mind and a proactive spirit.

David transitioned from insurance to the digital world, successfully becoming an online watchmaker, while Mark used his decades of experience in traditional sales to master digital marketing.

Both stories emphasize a key truth: whether you're crafting timepieces or digital strategies, your wealth of experience is a valuable asset.

For individuals over 50 considering a career pivot, these stories serve as a blueprint.

Combining your wealth of experience with new tech skills can redefine your professional trajectory.

Throughout the chapter, we've explored essential tools and strategies—AI, cybersecurity, social media, and e-commerce platforms—that create a robust framework for building a sustainable business.

Consider these elements the gears in a finely tuned machine, each playing a pivotal role in advancing your business vision.

But here's the key: it's about you taking that leap.

The digital world isn't just a labyrinth to navigate; it's a horizon brimming with potential for those ready to explore.

As we move to the next chapter, we'll focus on integrating these technologies into marketing strategies.

The goal is clear: master digital tools and engage more deeply with your audience, paving the way for lasting growth and success.

Embrace these strategies with enthusiasm, and let your journey be one of ongoing evolution, engagement, and excitement.

CHAPTER 5

MASTERING ONLINE MARKETING

You've set up your business, your product is ready, and you're prepared to tackle the tech terrain.

Now it's time to start marketing your new business online.

You're about to record your first video for social media.

What are your thoughts, your fears, and your ultimate goals?

Are you prepared?

Let's explore how others have found success.

It becomes easier with practice, and learning the basics can help ease your fears and hesitation.

INTRODUCTION: SETTING THE STAGE

In the digital age, online marketing is a transformative force for businesses.

Henry Blodget's story stands as a testament to the evolutionary power of online marketing.

Once a prominent figure on Wall Street, Blodget faced significant career challenges following a major setback within the financial industry.

However, he embraced digital strategies to rebuild his career from the ground up.

In 2007, Blodget co-founded Business Insider, a financial and business news website known for its insightful analysis and wide-ranging coverage of global business, technology, finance, politics, and lifestyle topics. It offered news articles, opinion pieces, and features that informed and engaged business professionals and general readers interested in understanding the dynamics of the business world.

By embracing a 'digital-first' strategy, Blodget harnessed the immense potential of online marketing, propelling Business Insider into a leading digital media outlet with a massive following.

Instead of relying on traditional print style of marketing, Blodget focused on delivering punchy, engaging content with compelling online headlines.

He skillfully employed SEO to boost visibility and rapidly shared content across multiple social media platforms, capturing the attention of a broad online audience.

His journey demonstrates that adversity can fuel innovation and success when paired with determination and adaptability.

Blodget's story exemplifies the core thesis of this chapter: the immense power of embracing online marketing to drive growth and resilience in business.

The digital landscape can indeed be daunting, but as Blodget demonstrates, it also offers unparalleled opportunities for those willing to harness its potential.

This story of reinvention serves as a guide for entrepreneurs seeking to enhance, grow, sustain, and scale their businesses through savvy online marketing.

Transitioning from Henry's inspiring journey, as we explore the essentials of online marketing, social media emerges as a pivotal starting point for connecting with audiences.

From social media strategies to email marketing, data analytics, and building online communities, this chapter equips you with tools to thrive and drive business growth in the digital world.

Let's explore how these platforms can be your launchpad for success.

SOCIAL MEDIA ESSENTIALS

Navigating the social media landscape can feel overwhelming for some and intimidating for others.

But when tackled with a clear plan, it becomes an indispensable tool for business growth.

Let's break it down platform by platform, each with its unique benefits and practical tips to help your business flourish.

Facebook: Building a Community

- Engage with Groups: Create or participate in Facebook groups related to your niche.

- Events and Live Videos: Organize online events or go live to interact directly with your audience, fostering a sense of community.

- Example: A local gym doubled its membership within a year by creating an active community group where members could share fitness tips and participate in challenges. Regular live Q&A sessions further engaged the community, fostering loyalty and attracting new members.

Instagram: Show, Don't Just Tell

- Visual Storytelling: Use Instagram Stories to show behind-the-scenes moments, product teasers, or customer testimonials.

- Consistency is Key: Schedule regular posts to maintain visibility and engagement by using Instagram's scheduling tools to plan your content in advance.

- Example: A boutique clothing brand increased online sales by 50% by posting daily Instagram Stories showcasing behind-the-scenes footage and customer testimonials. Their consistent use of visually compelling content helped maintain high visibility and engagement.

LinkedIn: Professional Growth

- Networking: Connect with professionals, share insights, and participate in industry discussions. LinkedIn is ideal for B2B interactions and for establishing authority in your field.

- Regular Updates: Keep your connections updated on your business's latest achievements or insights.

- Example: A B2B software company significantly expanded its reach by participating in industry discussions and sharing case studies. Regular updates on product innovations attracted new partnerships and enhanced its credibility within the tech community.

TikTok: Going Viral

- Creative Content: Use TikTok's format for creative challenges or tutorial videos that educate, entertain, and have the potential to go viral.

- Trend Participation: Stay on top of trending topics to ensure your content reaches a broader audience.

- Example: A small-town bakery increased foot traffic by 30% after sharing daily baking videos featuring creative tips. Their engaging content went viral, drawing a surge of new customers.

YouTube: Content-Rich Engagement

- Tutorials and Demos: Create in-depth videos that explain your products or services to help potential customers understand them more thoroughly.

- Series Format: Produce video series to deliver regular content and retain viewers.

- Example: A home improvement business boosted leads significantly by creating a series of comprehensive how-to videos. Their content educated viewers and positioned them as a trusted authority in DIY projects.

Strategic use of these platforms helps your business connect deeply with its audience, fostering loyalty and driving growth.

When used effectively, they can boost both your visibility and sales significantly.

While social media establishes a dynamic presence, email marketing serves as a powerful tool for deepening customer relationships and expanding your reach.

Reflection Question:

Which social media platform best aligns with your business goals?

Jot down three ideas to try this week.

Moving forward, let's simplify email marketing tactics to make them as effective and enjoyable to implement as our social media strategies.

Simplifying Email Marketing

Email marketing often feels like an overwhelming task with its many components, but breaking it down into manageable strategies can make it accessible and rewarding.

Let's simplify the process into three main pillars: building your list, segmenting your audience, and crafting compelling content.

1. Building Your List

   - Start by offering something valuable to potential subscribers. For example, you might provide a free e-book, an exclusive discount, or premium content tailored to their interests.

   - Use signup forms prominently on your website and social media to capture interested leads.

2. Segmenting Your Audience

   - To ensure your messages resonate, it's important to recognize that not all customers are the same. Divide your mailing list into segments based on interests, past purchases, or engagement levels.

   - Studies show that segmentation can increase email open rates by an impressive 203%, making it a game-changing strategy for email campaigns.

   - This tailored approach means you'll communicate more effectively, sending the right message to the right people at the right time.

3. Crafting Compelling Content

   - Your emails must capture attention instantly. Use compelling subject lines and craft content that aligns with your audience's interests.

- Personalize your emails — consider addressing recipients by name and including personalized recommendations.

- A successful example: a local gym increased class attendance by segmenting their audience by interest and sending personalized workout plans.

As you master these foundational elements of email marketing, they pave the way for more advanced strategies.

Consider John, a retired corporate executive, who grew a consulting business by leveraging email marketing.

He started sending out a monthly newsletter with strategic insights and industry updates, building a loyal audience and expanding his client base.

John built his email list by capturing addresses from those who requested more information. By delivering personalized, engaging content and tailored messaging, he not only connected with potential clients, but also established himself as a trusted thought leader in his industry.

With your audience beginning to grow, it's crucial to boost your online presence, increase your visibility, and draw in the ideal clients.

This is where Search Engine Optimization (SEO) and Search Engine Marketing (SEM) come into play, offering the strategies you need to achieve these objectives effectively.

SEO AND SEM SIMPLIFICATION

Search Engine Optimization (SEO) and Search Engine Marketing (SEM) are powerful tools that can significantly enhance your online presence.

Let's break down some beginner-friendly definitions and tactics

Definitions: SEO and SEM

- Search Engine Optimization (SEO) involves optimizing your website to achieve higher rankings in search engine results naturally, without paid ads.

- It involves using relevant keywords, improving website structure, and creating quality content that attracts and retains visitors.

- Search Engine Marketing (SEM) is a paid strategy to boost website visibility through search engine ads, targeting users actively searching for related products or services.

- It involves bidding on keywords to place ads in search engine results, targeting users actively searching for related products or services.

Armed with the insights from data analytics, you can better position your online marketing efforts to harness the full potential of SEO and SEM strategies.

SEO Basics

1. Keyword Research:

- Definition: Keywords are the specific words or phrases users type into search engines when searching for information, products, or services.

- How-To: Utilize tools like Google Keyword Planner or SEMrush to discover popular and relevant search terms aligned with your business goals.

- Example: If you own a vegan bakery, keywords might include "vegan cupcakes" or "plant-based desserts."

2. Optimized Meta Descriptions:

- Definition: A meta description is a brief summary of your webpage content that appears in search results.

- How-To: Ensure each page on your site has a unique, engaging meta description with relevant keywords.

- Example: "Discover the best vegan cupcakes made fresh daily with organic ingredients."

SEM Basics

1. Setting Up a Google Ads Campaign:

- Step 1: Create a Google Ads account.

- Step 2: Define your campaign goal (e.g., website visits, sales).

- Step 3: Choose your target audience based on demographics and interests.

- Step 4: Select appropriate keywords from your research.

- Step 5: Write compelling ad copy that highlights your unique selling points, uses action-oriented language, and includes relevant keywords.

- Step 6: Establish a clear budget, determine the duration of your campaign, and launch it to reach your target audience.

2. Monitor and Optimize:

- Regularly track your ad performance.

- Make adjustments to improve results, such as tweaking keywords or updating ad copy.

With your search engine strategies in place, you're better equipped to capture your audience's attention and boost your business's visibility.

After launching your email campaigns and search engine strategies, the next crucial step is to measure their performance. Data analytics helps you identify what works and refine your efforts for maximum impact.

So let's discover how data analytics can fine-tune your marketing efforts and unlock new opportunities for growth and sustainability.

LEVERAGING DATA ANALYTICS

In today's digital age, understanding the role of data is key for small businesses looking to elevate their online marketing game.

But don't let data analytics intimidate you—think of it as a tool to better understand your customers.

Using tools like Google Analytics and A/B testing, you can refine your strategies to maximize impact and increase audience engagement.

Understanding Data Analytics

- Google Analytics: This essential tool provides detailed insights into how customers interact with your website, including metrics like page views, session duration, and bounce rates. Through the use of this tool, you can better understand your audience and pinpoint areas for improvement.

- A/B Testing: This method compares two variations of your web content to identify which performs better, allowing you to optimize elements like headlines, images, and layouts based on data-driven insights.

- Whether it's tweaking headlines, images, or layouts, this method provides concrete data to guide your marketing decisions and optimize audience engagement.

Fictional Case Study: Jane's Crafts

Jane runs a small online craft store and wants to increase her sales.

Using Google Analytics, Jane discovers that most visitors exit her site after viewing the homepage, indicating a need for improvement in design and engagement.

With these insights, she decides to conduct A/B testing on her homepage layout and call-to-action (CTA) button text.

After testing a more engaging CTA and showcasing her best-selling products prominently on the homepage, Jane achieves a 20% increase in sales conversions within a month.

Key Steps for Beginners:

1. Set Clear Objectives: Clearly define your data goals, such as increasing conversion rates, enhancing user experience, and identifying customer preferences.

2. Leverage Google Analytics:

   a. Initiate Setup: Ensure Google Analytics is properly installed on your website to start collecting valuable data.

   b. Focus on High-Traffic Pages: Pinpoint the pages with the highest visitor numbers, then evaluate their content, design, and user flow to uncover areas for improvement.

   c. Monitor Regularly: Consistently check metrics aligned with your business objectives, and track trends and improvements on a weekly basis.

3. Conduct A/B Testing: Test one variable at a time (e.g., button color, headline) to understand what changes drive positive user engagement.

By mastering data analytics, small business owners can refine their marketing approaches, resulting in improved user engagement and sales.

Reflection Question:

What key metric would you want to track to use data analytics to gain a deeper understanding of your audience and the needs and desires to help you refine your marketing efforts?

Consider using a tool like Google Analytics to start collecting data based on this metric.

Transitioning forward, the next step is to focus on crafting compelling content that captivates and resonates with your audience.

Let's explore how to take it to the next level by creating engaging content that resonates with your audience and strengthens your online marketing efforts.

CREATING ENGAGING CONTENT

In today's digital landscape, content that resonates with audiences is essential for any thriving business.

Engaging content thrives on storytelling—a powerful tool that transforms casual viewers into devoted customers by fostering emotional connections.

Consider a brand like TOMS Shoes. Their "One for One" campaign transcended selling shoes by weaving a story of social responsibility, linking every purchase to a meaningful cause: giving back to underserved communities.

This approach not only humanized their brand but also created a passionate customer base eager to participate in their mission.

Equally important in crafting engaging content is leveraging the voices of your customers through user-generated content.

Encouraging customers to share their experiences adds authenticity and builds trust.

This is a strategy that Starbucks used. They routinely feature customer photos in their marketing campaigns.

This not only boosts engagement but also reinforces a sense of community around the brand.

Key Elements of Engaging Content:

Storytelling:

- Craft compelling narratives that showcase your brand's values and forge emotional connections with your audience.

User-Generated Content:

- Encourage customers to share their stories and highlight these in your marketing efforts.

Consistency:

- Create a content calendar to ensure a consistent flow of fresh, relevant material that keeps your audience engaged.

While storytelling lays the foundation for engagement, the next step involves creating dynamic, interactive experiences that captivate your audience. It extends into how you create conversations and build interactive experiences.

Let's explore how tools like quizzes and polls can deepen customer engagement and drive growth in an online business.

Interactive Content

Integrating interactive content into your marketing strategy can elevate engagement levels and build stronger connections with your audience.

Here's how you can begin:

Quizzes and Polls: These are effective tools for engaging users and gaining insights into their preferences.

- Example: A local coffee shop designs a fun quiz on their website titled 'Find Your Perfect Brew,' engaging coffee enthusiasts while gathering insights into their preferences.

Live Q&A Sessions: Hosting live sessions on platforms like Instagram or Facebook allows you to interact with your audience in real-time.

- Example: Imagine a fashion boutique hosting a live Q&A session once a week, discussing the latest trends and answering customer questions. This can create a sense of community and keep the audience coming back.

Interactive Video Content: Use platforms like YouTube to enhance engagement by adding clickable elements or choices in the video.

- Example: A cooking channel offers interactive video recipes where viewers can choose different ingredients to see various outcomes.

Case Study: Fictional Boutique

Let's consider Style Loft, a fictional fashion boutique.

Style Loft launched an interactive quiz on their website, 'Find Your Fashion Persona,' which invited users to discover their unique style through engaging questions.

The quiz not only attracted new visitors but also encouraged the participants to share their results on social media platforms, increasing the boutique's online visibility.

Simultaneously, Style Loft initiated monthly Instagram live sessions, offering personalized style tips and fostering direct engagement with their followers.

This approach not only boosted brand loyalty but also enhanced customer satisfaction as they felt more connected to the brand.

While individual interactions are crucial for engagement, the real power lies in building online communities that turn loyal customers into brand advocates.

But taking the engagement strategy to the next level is the power of building communities,

Developing online communities can become the backbone of your marketing efforts, turning loyal customers into brand advocates.

So let's discover how to create and nurture these communities effectively.

DEVELOPING ONLINE COMMUNITIES

Creating an engaged online community can become the cornerstone of your business, driving loyalty and amplifying your brand's impact.

By fostering a sense of belonging and connection, you can cultivate a loyal base of customers and advocates who support and spread your brand's mission.

Tips for Fostering Meaningful Interactions:

- Be Authentic and Present: Demonstrate genuine interest by actively participating in conversations and promptly addressing feedback from community members.

- Encourage User Participation: Create spaces for dialogue, such as forums or live chats, where members can share their thoughts and experiences.

- Offer Value: Offer exclusive content, early product access, or special promotions as perks to reward and nurture your community members. This nurtures a feeling of appreciation and belonging.

Case Study: Brand X's Success Story

Take, for example, Brand X, a boutique clothing company that cultivated a thriving online community centered on sustainable fashion.

Through a dedicated Facebook Group, Brand X fostered discussions on eco-friendly practices and while highlighting inspiring customer stories.

This strategy not only solidified Brand X's identity as a leader in sustainable fashion, but also boosted customer retention by 30%. Members felt they were part of a larger movement, further reinforcing their loyalty to Brand X.

As we conclude our discussion on online communities, it's time to synthesize these insights into a roadmap for effective online marketing.

CONCLUSION: TYING IT TOGETHER

As this chapter concludes, it's evident that today's digital landscape presents a wealth of tools and strategies to drive your business growth.

Social media platforms provide an essential launchpad for audience engagement and growth, while email marketing builds and fortifies customer relationships.

Through the power of data analytics, you can refine your strategies, and with SEO and SEM, amplify your visibility to reach the right people.

Crafting engaging content fosters deeper connections with your audience and builds brand loyalty.

By embracing online marketing, you equip your business not only to survive but to thrive in our increasingly digital world.

Much like Henry Blodget, who revitalized his career through strategic digital engagement, you too can harness these tools to drive success.

Remember, the essence of mastering online marketing lies in continuous learning and adaptation.

Each element weaves together to form a cohesive strategy that can sustain and scale your business.

Now is the time to take action.

Start by selecting one strategy from this chapter to implement today. Even a single step forward can lead to monumental growth in your business journey.

It's now time to shift our focus to taking these marketing insights and strategies, and turning them into an actionable launch plan, applying the tips outlined in this chapter:

Quick Action Plan:

Start Today:

Choose a single social media platform to focus your efforts on, and commit to a 30-day plan to explore its features and engage with your audience.

Engage with your audience and explore the features that the social media platform offers.

Compose Your Message:

Write a concise, impactful email for your mailing list, ensuring the message is clear, engaging, and tailored to your subscribers' needs.

Evaluate Your Visibility:

Leverage a free SEO tool to assess your website's performance, identify opportunities for improvement, and optimize for better visibility with your target audience.

Examples of free SEO tools include Google Search Console for monitoring website performance, Google Analytics for tracking visitor behavior, and Screaming Frog SEO Spider for detailed site audits.

Integrating marketing strategies into your business launch will not only set a solid foundation for your business, but also propel your business toward success.

Prepare to put your newfound knowledge into action as we embark on the next chapter—crafting a comprehensive business launch plan that transforms strategies into tangible results.

CHAPTER 6

CREATING A WINNING LAUNCH PLAN

INTRODUCTION: EMILY'S LAUNCH JOURNEY

Launching a business is like embarking on an expedition—brimming with excitement, anticipation, and moments of uncertainty.

Emily, an aspiring entrepreneur, stood on the brink of her dreams, her heart a blend of excitement and apprehension.

Emily's journey is one that many aspiring entrepreneurs will find relatable.

Emily, a mid-level professional in her late 50s, has been an avid reader for years. She discovered her passion for sustainable urban gardening this way, realizing she could transform her hobby into a thriving landscape design business.

Her journey began with a simple idea: combining her passion for sustainable urban gardening with her insight into unmet needs in the landscape design market.

She knew her vision had the potential to transform into a thriving business, and was excited about creating a side hustle business in her free time based on her passion for gardening.

Like many new entrepreneurs, Emily grappled with the daunting challenge of bringing her unique vision to life in a competitive market.

She experienced many sleepless nights, exploring ways to overcome the challenge of defining a distinctive brand identity.

Yet Emily's journey wasn't defined by obstacles alone—it was a story of transformation and growth.

With meticulous preparation and steadfast dedication, Emily refined her strategies, channeling her passion into a flourishing landscape design business.

Her journey demonstrates that success isn't just about having a brilliant idea—it's about thoroughly understanding your audience, crafting a strategy that resonates, and continuously evolving through each challenge faced.

Emily's evolution from a hopeful dreamer to a strategic entrepreneur serves as a framework for what any reader can achieve with persistence and the right launch plan.

In this chapter, we'll explore the key components of building a successful launch plan tailored to your goals.

By integrating comprehensive marketing strategies and operational logistics, your business can not only make a successful debut but also ensure growth and scalability.

As you continue reading, let Emily's story inspire you as a reminder of what's possible with determination and the right strategy.

Although many people fear that as we age, it's harder to become successful learning new skills and starting a new business from scratch.

Yet, a 2019 study by the Kauffman Foundation found that over 25% of new entrepreneurs were between ages 55 and 64.

The foundation also found that entrepreneurs over 50 are nearly twice as likely to succeed as their younger counterparts due to their experience and networks.

Launching a business can feel overwhelming, especially when starting later in life.

But as Emily's story shows, the right plan can transform uncertainty into opportunity, and it's never too late to start.

For Emily, the road to a successful launch began long before the product hit the market, and with her experience and determination, she was able to find the success she hoped for.

Next, we'll delve into understanding your audience and preparing your market entry—two foundational steps that set the stage for long-term success.

These crucial elements can set the tone for your business's growth trajectory and long-term success.

AUDIENCE AND MARKET PREPARATION

CUSTOMER PERSONAS

Understanding your audience is crucial to a successful launch.

Imagine knowing your customers so well that every message you craft resonates with them.

This is where customer personas come in.

To create customer personas, explore demographic data, analyze behaviors, and identify the challenges your ideal clients face.

For example, if you're launching a consulting business, a persona might be:

"Susan, 55, is a mid-level manager transitioning to freelancing. She values flexibility, prioritizes clear communication, and seeks time-saving resources."

Here's how Emily did it.

She began by surveying her followers, analyzing their feedback, and categorizing them into segments based on shared characteristics.

This process deepened her understanding of her audience and guided her marketing strategies to better align with their needs and preferences.

Actionable Steps:

- Conduct surveys or interviews to gather insights about your audience.

- Use tools like Google Analytics to find demographic information.

- Group your audience into categories based on shared interests, needs, or common traits.

- (This is often called "segmenting" your audience.)

Consider Adam, 62, a CPA with a lifelong passion for woodworking, looking for a side hustle that allowed him to earn added income while sharing the joy of his hobby with others.

By getting to know and understanding his audience's preferences for handmade, quality products, and using his knowledge and experience as a CPA, he successfully launched and grew an Etsy story into a booming business.

Once you understand your audience, the next step is to analyze your competition to find opportunities where your business can excel.

COMPETITIVE ANALYSIS

Understanding your competitors helps you identify market gaps and differentiate your business effectively.

A SWOT Analysis is a helpful tool used to identify and evaluate the Strengths, Weaknesses, Opportunities, and Threats of a business or project.

This analysis helps businesses understand their internal capabilities and external possibilities to make informed strategic decisions.

For example, Emily conducted a SWOT analysis to uncover her strengths and market opportunities, refining her strategy to stand out in the competitive landscape.

The analysis revealed areas where she could offer more value or present a unique perspective, positioning her business to stand out in the market.

Actionable Steps:

- Start by identifying who's serving your audience today.

- Explore what makes their offerings work - and where you could do even better.

- Perform a SWOT analysis to determine where you have a competitive edge.

- Identify gaps in the market that your value proposition can fill.

VALUE PROPOSITION

Your value proposition is your commitment to your customers—a clear explanation of why your product is the ideal choice.

Emily refined her value proposition by highlighting the unique benefits of her service, emphasizing both the emotional and practical advantages for her customers.

This was not just a statement of features but a compelling narrative that positioned her brand as indispensable.

Actionable Steps: Take a moment to draft your own value proposition.

- Begin by identifying what makes your product or service unique.

- What unique benefits does your product or service offer to your customers?

- Consider how your product addresses a specific need or problem for your audience?

- Test different messaging to see what resonates best with your audience.

- Make your value proposition concise, clear, and prominently displayed across all marketing materials to ensure maximum visibility and impact.

With a clear understanding of your audience and market, you are now poised to strategically time your launch.

Let's explore how being aligned with seasonal trends and events can amplify your reach and ensure your debut is not just noticed, but celebrated.

This planning sets the stage for a successful business debut, facilitating growth and scalability in the next section, "Timing and Strategy."

TIMING AND STRATEGY

BUILDING YOUR EMAIL LIST

Building a strong email list is a foundational step in crafting an effective email marketing strategy.

Start by offering value to potential subscribers, such as a free e-book or exclusive discount, encouraging them to provide their email addresses in return.

Expand your reach by leveraging your existing network and promoting your offer on social media platforms.

- Goal: Build an engaged community ready for your product launch.

- Tip: Use social proof and testimonials to enhance trust and persuade more sign-ups.

SEGMENTING THE AUDIENCE

After establishing your list, the next crucial step is audience segmentation.

This means categorizing the subscribers based on interests, past behaviors, or demographic information.

By doing so, you ensure that the right message reaches the right people at the right time.

- Goal: Tailor personalized content to resonate with the unique preferences and interests of each audience segment.

- Tip: Use behavior tracking to understand your audience better and tailor your messages effectively.

CRAFTING COMPELLING CONTENT

The cornerstone of an effective email strategy lies in crafting compelling, value-driven content that captivates and informs your audience.

Each email should do one of three things: tell a story, offer insights, or offer exclusive deals.

Prioritize clear and concise messaging designed to inspire immediate action.

- Goal: Engage your audience and drive them toward your product.

- Tip: Use eye-catching visuals and strong call-to-actions (CTAs) to increase engagement and clicks.

Successful Email Campaign Example

Take Brand XYZ's as an example: they successfully launched an eco-friendly product by strategically building and segmenting their email list, tailoring content to emphasize its environmental benefits.

Their emails featured testimonials and behind-the-scenes stories, which resulted in a 40% increase in conversions on launch day.

As you prepare your email marketing strategies, remember that timing is key.

Ensuring your messages reach your audience when they're most attentive can bolster engagement.

Meet Linda, a 57-year-old corporate executive with a flair for event organization.

Driven to transform her passion into a thriving side consulting business, Linda leveraged her extensive network to build a powerful email list.

She strategically grouped ("segmented") her contacts based on their potential interest in hosting special events.

She crafted engaging, compelling content tailored to each audience group and timed her emails precisely for a few months before the holidays, just when her audience starts planning events.

This strategy not only attracted potential clients, but also established a loyal customer base, enabling Linda to realize her vision of creating a thriving special-events consultation business.

Now that you've mastered understanding your audience and having developed effective marketing timing strategies, let's turn to pre-launch activities.

It's time to generate buzz that captivates and sets the stage for strong growth and grabs attention right from the start.

Creating Pre-Launch Buzz - A Step-by-Step Teaser Campaign Guide

TEASER CAMPAIGN TIMELINE

Week 1: Building Curiosity

- Social Media Posts: Share cryptic images, quotes, and questions related to your brand's mission to intrigue your audience.

- Email Teasers: Send a "something exciting is coming" email to your list. Include a countdown to build anticipation.

- Blog Post: Publish an article hinting at upcoming changes or innovations, highlighting what viewers should look forward to.

Week 2: Create Engagement

- Interactive Polls/Quizzes: Utilize social media stories to engage your audience with fun, brand-related polls or quizzes.

- Sneak Peek Video: Release a short, behind-the-scenes video that hints at what's next without revealing too much.

- Email Update: Encourage your audience to engage by asking for their opinions on potential features or offerings.

Week 3: Build Speculation

- Mystery Collaborations: Announce a partnership without providing full details, keep the collaboration under wraps.

- Exclusive Group Teaser: Offer a special group (like a Facebook group or Discord channel) a first look, encouraging members to speculate.

- Email Preview: Share a visual or audio clip that teases what's to come, sparking discussions.

Week 4: Final Push

- Social Takeover: Have a key influencer or team member take over your social media to share their excitement and experiences.

- Countdown Videos: Post daily countdown videos with a mix of behind-the-scenes snippets and team member testimonials.

- Final Email Blast: Announce exactly what's launching, highlighting why it's worth the wait and including a strong call-to-action for launch day.

Following this guide, you've carefully built anticipation through your strategic teaser campaign.

By the end of Week 4, your audience should feel eager and ready to engage with your product on launch day.

It's now time to deepen your connection with your audience.

By sharing behind-the-scenes insights, you can humanize your brand, making it relatable and inspiring trust.

Behind-the-Scenes Insights

Sharing behind-the-scenes glimpses can forge meaningful connections with your audience, enhancing your brand's relatability and trustworthiness.

While entertaining, behind-the-scenes insights also serve as a strategic tool to reinforce your brand's authenticity and foster relatability.

One way to accomplish this is to post short-form videos that give behind the scenes looks at your business process or a story about the "why" behind the start of your business (e.g. your calling and what you hope to accomplish, helping others).

Humanizing the Brand

Sharing the authentic stories behind your business—its challenges, triumphs, and daily operations—humanizes your brand and makes it more relatable.

Customers connect on a personal level when they witness the genuine effort and passion behind your product or service.

This transparency fosters trust and makes your brand more relatable, turning prospects into loyal customers who feel invested in your journey.

Building Emotional Connections

Building emotional connections is fundamental to cultivate lasting customer relationships.

By sharing behind-the-scenes content, you invite people into your world, allowing them to experience the emotions driving your business.

By sharing heartfelt stories, team moments, and authentic narratives, you foster a sense of belonging and alignment with your brand's core values.

Engaging Audiences with Interactive Content

Interactive content, like live Q&A sessions and virtual workspace tours, directly engages your audience, drawing them into your brand's narrative.

Engagement tools not only entertain but also educate, allowing your audience to participate and connect in real-time.

Such interaction fosters brand loyalty, builds a community atmosphere, and promotes organic growth through word-of-mouth recommendations.

With these genuine connections established, it's time to shift focus toward crafting a grand entrance that will captivate your audience.

As you prepare for the big unveiling, think about crafting a strategy that not only captures but also maintains the interest of your audience. This reinforces the essential function of online marketing in successfully launching and expanding your business.

PREPARATION FOR A GRAND ENTRANCE

Planning a memorable launch requires attention to detail, creativity, and strategic execution.

As you prepare to unveil your passion project to the world, it's vital to ensure every element of your launch is carefully orchestrated for maximum impact.

This section will guide you through a step-by-step checklist to draft a compelling press release, choose the right influencers, and plan a launch event that leaves a lasting impression.

Get ready to captivate your audience and make a statement that underscores the significance of your business debut.

Step-by-Step Checklist

Crafting a Press Release:

- Headline: Craft a headline that succinctly captures the essence of your announcement and grabs attention.

- Introduction: Write a strong opening that answers the who, what, where, when, and why.

- Body: Provide detailed information, including quotes from key stakeholders.

- Contact Information: Include your contact details for further inquiries.

- Boilerplate: Conclude with a concise overview of your brand or business to provide context.

Selecting Influencers:

- Research: Find influencers whose values, content, and audience demographics align with your brand.

- Engagement Rate: Evaluate potential influencers based on their audience engagement rates.

- Content Style: Ensure the influencer's content style matches your brand image.

- Partnership Terms: Outline expectations, compensation, and campaign goals clearly.

Planning a Launch Event:

- Venue Selection: Choose a location that resonates with your brand identity.

- Guest List: Invite key stakeholders, media personnel, and influencers.

- Event Agenda: Design an agenda with engaging activities, like live demonstrations or Q&A sessions, to spotlight your product or service.

- Promotion: Utilize social media and email newsletters to promote the event and encourage attendance.

- Follow-up: Plan for post-event engagement with attendees to maintain momentum.

As you finalize preparations for your grand entrance, it's crucial to align every detail with your overarching strategy. Leveraging the power of online marketing will transform your launch from a single event into a catalyst for sustainable growth.

You've already laid the groundwork for a lasting impression on your audience.

Now, the focus shifts to maximizing the momentum you've created.

Next, we'll delve into post-launch strategies that harness the power of online marketing to drive sustained growth and scalability.

This helps ensure your business continues to flourish beyond its debut.

POST-LAUNCH STRATEGIES

The post launch phase is just as critical to a business's success as preparation leading up to the reveal.

During this phase, entrepreneurs must focus on gathering and analyzing early feedback. These insights are invaluable for shaping future strategies and informed decision-making.

Leveraging this feedback allows you to pivot, adapt, and ultimately grow stronger.

Consider Slack, a company that wholeheartedly embraced user feedback.

Initially designed for internal use, Slack meticulously analyzed user suggestions and complaints, leveraging feedback to evolve into the indispensable communication tool it is today.

The Importance of Early Feedback

Gathering Initial Reactions:

- Systematically collect data through surveys, polls, and direct customer feedback.

- Encourage detailed and honest reviews by offering incentives, such as future purchase discounts.

Analyzing Feedback for Insights:

- Look for recurring themes and patterns in the feedback to uncover actionable insights.

- Use these insights to make informed decisions about product improvements or marketing strategies.

Implementing Changes:

- Prioritize changes that offer the highest value to your audience.

- Communicate to your audience that their feedback is appreciated and being acted upon.

Iterative Improvements:

- Continuously refine and enhance your product using ongoing customer feedback.

- Maintain an open dialogue with your customers, showing them that their opinions matter.

With a strong foundation established through post-launch refinements and adaptive strategies, we now transition to a reflective close.

The journey you've embarked on doesn't just end here; it evolves, celebrating the strength of thoughtful online marketing to elevate and expand your business.

By building a robust foundation through detailed customer personas, identifying and articulating a clear value proposition, and developing a strategic launch plan, you set your business up for a successful debut.

These components not only guide your initial launch but also provide a framework for ongoing growth and adaptation.

By understanding your market, differentiating effectively from competitors, and fostering deep engagement with your audience through online marketing, you equip your business with the tools for enduring success.

CONCLUSION: HARNESSING THE POWER OF ONLINE MARKETING

As we conclude this chapter, let Emily's journey serve as inspiration.

Her story exemplifies the transformative power of strategic online marketing, propelling a business from concept to successful launch and beyond.

By crafting a comprehensive launch plan, engaging meaningfully with her audience, and embracing adaptability, Emily transformed challenges into stepping stones on her path to success.

Incorporating these strategies into your business launch isn't merely about following steps; it's about adopting a mindset focused on growth, adaptability, and continuous learning.

Every lesson here is a tool to help you scale and sustain your business—now it's time to put these plans into action.

Reflection Questions and Call To Action:

Reflect on your unique skills and passions.

- What problem can you solve for your ideal customer, and how does it align with their needs?

Before moving forward, ask yourself:

- Have I defined my ideal customer persona?

- Have I identified gaps in the market?

- Have I clearly articulated my unique value proposition?

Remember, it's never too late to start—many successful entrepreneurs in the U.S. began their businesses at age 50 or later!

Your path to success is shaped by the decisions you make today.

As we move to the next chapter—focused on overcoming the challenges of being a new entrepreneur—carry forward this knowledge and confidence to navigate and conquer whatever lies ahead.

You're on the path to becoming well-equipped to turn your business dreams into reality.

CHAPTER 7

OVERCOMING BUDDING ENTREPRENEUR CHALLENGES

INTRODUCTION: MEET ANNETTE—A JOURNEY THROUGH CHALLENGES

Imagine dedicating years to one career, only to pivot to something entirely new in your 50's or beyond, driven by a newfound interest or a longstanding passion.

Along the way, you encounter unforeseen challenges.

That's exactly what Annette faced—and conquered.

Annette, 55 years old, with a background in teaching, was passionate about education and had always dreamed of building an online tutoring platform that could reach students worldwide.

However, turning her dream into reality was riddled with unexpected hurdles.

Like many budding entrepreneurs, Annette's initial enthusiasm collided with the cold realities of tech glitches, marketing missteps, and operational overload.

OVERCOMING TECH GLITCHES

Early on, Annette encountered a series of technical challenges that almost derailed her project. Her website frequently crashed and lacked a user-friendly interface.

Refusing to let these hurdles stop her, Annette reached out to tech forums and networked with IT professionals. These connections helped guide her through the obstacles, offering valuable insights and solutions.

Inspired by stories like Spotify's Daniel Ek, who faced similar challenges with streaming, Annette chose to hire a skilled developer. Soon, her website was transformed into a stable, customer-friendly platform.

With her technical challenges now under control and her platform running smoothly, Annette turned her attention to the next hurdle: reaching her target audience in the complex world of marketing.

NAVIGATING MARKETING MISSTEPS

Marketing became Annette's next big challenge. In her 50s, with teaching, she knew people and understood her audience, but had no real experience with marketing.

Her early campaigns failed to connect with the right audience.

Determined to learn from the best, she studied successful marketing stories, like those behind Slack, to reshape her strategy.

Slack's marketing story was largely centered around using word-of-mouth marketing, and allowed users to easily try the product.

This customer-centric approach encouraged people to adopt the platform quickly and the word about Slack spread within networks.

This led to a rapid growth of the company without having to rely on traditional, often expensive, marketing campaigns.

Annette realized her ideal audience - often busy parents - valued quick convenient solutions.

In response, she refined her value proposition (her tutoring offer) and highlighted the benefits to parents in her marketing.

As a result, by leveraging social media platforms and gathering feedback through surveys, she crafted messages that resonated, resulting in a 40% increase in engagement and user registrations.

TACKLING OPERATIONAL WORKLOAD

Annette soon found the operational side of running a business overwhelming.

Juggling roles from customer support to finance stretched her thin.

By following advice from productivity experts and using project management tools like Trello, Annette streamlined her workflow.

By delegating tasks through freelance platforms, Annette was able to focus on strategic growth, significantly reducing her workload stress.

BUILDING RESILIENCE THROUGH STRATEGIC SOLUTIONS

Throughout her journey, Annette demonstrated strategic problem-solving.

She applied agile principles, focusing on iterative improvements and maintaining flexibility in her approach.

Annette's story is a testament to the power of resilience and adaptability—the cornerstone of her entrepreneurial success.

Annette's journey is a vivid illustration of the fact that no entrepreneurial path is free from obstacles.

Her ability to transform setbacks into stepping stones reminds every beginner that while the entrepreneurial landscape is challenging, it is also fertile ground for growth.

Using Annette's story as an example of resilience and adaptability despite challenges in business, let's explore what specific challenges are common among new entrepreneurs and how recognizing these can equip you to better plan and navigate your own venture successfully.

This will lay the groundwork for building the resilience and developing the problem-solving strategies essential for keeping your new business venture on track.

IDENTIFYING COMMON CHALLENGES FOR NEW EN-TREPRENEURS

NAVIGATING THE INITIAL STORMS

Embarking on the entrepreneurial journey can often feel like setting sail in uncharted waters.

Every new entrepreneur, like our fictional Emily and real-life Annette, faces a range of obstacles and challenges that, when identified, can be tackled with foresight, ingenuity, and strategic planning.

From technological hurdles to emotional rollercoasters, the path is fraught with potential pitfalls.

COMMON HURDLES

Every budding entrepreneur encounters a set of universal trials during their startup phase. Here are some of the most common challenges:

Tech Troubles:

- Navigating the digital landscape can be daunting.

- Many new entrepreneurs struggle with building user-friendly websites or integrating secure e-commerce solutions.

- For instance, Annette faced significant tech challenges in launching her tutoring platform.

- She tackled these by investing in tech support and educating herself on necessary digital tools.

Marketing Misalignments:

- Understanding your market is crucial.

- Like Emily, many entrepreneurs launch without a clear target audience or a compelling value proposition.

- To rectify this, study successful businesses like Slack, which excelled by learning from user feedback and adjusting their marketing strategies accordingly.

Operational Overload:

- Balancing multiple roles—from finance to customer service—can be overwhelming.

- Employing task management tools and prioritizing tasks, as Annette did, can alleviate this burden, allowing you to focus on growth.

Financial Constraints:

- According to various reviews, 60-75% of people over 50 who fund new business ventures as 'encore entrepreneurs' primarily use their personal savings to start their ventures.

- This practice is commonly referred to as 'bootstrapping'— funding their businesses without seeking external support.

- Misjudging startup costs is a common mistake, so developing a comprehensive financial plan is often advised.

- This should include consideration of both initial and ongoing expenses.

- One of the tools commonly used is QuickBooks for tracking.

EMOTIONAL CHALLENGES AND OVERCOMING SELF-DOUBT

Beyond logistical challenges, new entrepreneurs often face emotional barriers like fear of failure and self-doubt.

These emotions can halt progress, making it crucial to develop strategies for emotional resilience.

For example, a woman in her 50s who had spent years working for others, found herself doubting her ability to lead when she started her own business.

To counter these feelings, she started a weekly journaling practice, documenting her achievements and reflecting on lessons learned from setbacks.

She established a morning routine with mindfulness and goal-setting to reduce self-doubt and stay focused.

This routine not only boosted her confidence, but also kept her focused and motivated on her business goals.

Recognizing these emotions as part of the entrepreneurial journey, rather than obstacles, and addressing them proactively, can lead to sustained progress and success.

Here are a few techniques or strategies to overcome common fears and self-doubts:

Acknowledge Your Fears:

- Recognize that fear is a normal part of the journey. Begin by identifying your specific fears.

- Are they related to market acceptance? Financial viability?

- Reflect on these fears to understand their roots.

Build a Support Network:

- Surround yourself with mentors and peers who can offer guidance and reassurance.

- For example, Annette found strength in her network, which provided both practical advice and emotional support.

Goal Setting & Positive Reinforcement:

- Set achievable goals to create a sense of accomplishment and progress.

- Celebrate small wins to boost confidence and motivate continued effort.

Reflect and Adapt:

- Regularly assess your strategies.

- Ask yourself, "What went well this week? What didn't? What can I improve?"

- Use setbacks as learning opportunities rather than roadblocks.

Understanding these initial challenges is the first step in laying a strong foundation for your entrepreneurial venture.

The next step is to equip yourself with a toolkit of strategic solutions that can transform those challenges into opportunities for success.

STRATEGIC SOLUTIONS: TURNING OBSTACLES INTO OPPORTUNITIES

In entrepreneurship, challenges often present the most critical opportunities to learn and grow.

Let's explore some strategic problem-solving approaches that you can apply to transform obstacles into stepping stones for success:

Agile Thinking for Flexibility

Agile thinking is like navigating a maze—you adjust your path with each turn, staying flexible and focused on your goal."

This involves breaking down tasks into smaller, manageable components, allowing you to respond swiftly to changes or setbacks.

For instance, if facing a tech issue, rather than being overwhelmed, tackle it step-by-step with regular check-ins on progress.

ACTION EXERCISE:

Regularly review your project goals.

Adapt them based on new insights and feedback from customers and audience.

This keeps you aligned with current market demands.

Systems Thinking

See your challenges as part of a larger system instead of isolated incidents.

Adopting a systems thinking approach means viewing challenges as interconnected.

Identify root causes and bottlenecks, uncovering opportunities for improvement.

For example, if your marketing efforts fall short, consider how client feedback, team dynamics, or market conditions may be affecting the results.

Quick Exercise:

Map out a current challenge you're facing.

See how it connects with other areas of your business.

This visual can help uncover new strategies.

Leveraging Resources

Effective problem-solving thrives on resourcefulness.

Engage with platforms like GlowUp, known for collaborative problem-solving, and seek advice from stakeholders for fresh insights and potential solutions.

Tip: Join online forums or business communities to gain access to diverse ideas and strategies.

Capability Enhancement

Continuously develop both your skills and those of your team.

For example, learning a new software can streamline operations or improve service delivery.

Use platforms like LinkedIn Learning for resources to stay updated and competitive.

Checklist for Growth:

- Identify areas where you or your team can improve, such as learning new software or streamlining processes.

- Set learning targets for yourself and your employees.

- Close gaps with online courses or workshops

As you turn obstacles and challenges into opportunities, remember that entrepreneurship requires balancing emotional resilience with strategic skills.

Building resilience is key to navigating the inevitable ups and downs, and learning from failure is a powerful step towards long-term success.

Let's explore how you can cultivate this crucial mindset to keep your business venture on track.

EMOTIONAL RESILIENCE AND LEARNING FROM FAILURE

Becoming an entrepreneur is inherently emotional, filled with highs and lows that can often feel overwhelming. For every exhilarating step forward, there might be moments of self-doubt and fear of failure.

Emotional resilience is like your secret weapon. It's what keeps you moving forward when everything feels like it's pulling you back.

Annette, for instance, faced numerous moments of feeling overwhelmed, with self-doubt and fear of failure. However, she was resilient. She smartly delegated tasks by leveraging freelance platforms, allowing her to focus on strategic growth and significantly reducing her workload stress.

It's important to acknowledge these feelings as part of the journey rather than obstacles.

Here are some strategies to manage these emotions and maintain your momentum.

1. Embrace Your Emotions:

Recognize that feeling overwhelmed or anxious is natural when venturing into the unknown.

These emotions are not signs of weakness but signals that you're pushing beyond your comfort zone.

2. Start Small and Celebrate Wins:

Breaking down your goals into smaller tasks can make the enormous feel achievable.

Celebrate even the smallest victories and regularly remind yourself of how far you've come—each win is a stepping stone toward your larger vision.

These small successes provide the motivation and confidence needed to tackle bigger challenges.

Like Annette, who cherished each successful tutoring session as a milestone, acknowledge your accomplishments, no matter how minor they might seem.

3. Build a Support System:

Whether it's a mentor, an accountability partner, or a supportive community, surround yourself with people who can offer guidance and reassurance.

Sharing your journey can offer you new perspectives, encouragement, and reassurance that you're not alone. It's invaluable to have a network that celebrates your wins and supports you through setbacks.

For instance, when Annette felt lost, she reached out to a fellow entrepreneur who had faced similar issues and found invaluable support.

4. Shift Your Perspective on Failure (Positive Reframing):

Redefine failure as an opportunity to learn and grow.

Each setback offers insights into what didn't work and why—information that can be crucial for your next steps.

Ask yourself, "What can I learn from this setback?"

This approach can turn fear into a steppingstone for growth.

View failure as a temporary state, and use it as an opportunity to learn and grow in a new direction.

This will empower you to innovate and experiment with new strategies.

Practical Steps to Boost Confidence and Manage Stress:

- Mindfulness Practices: Practice daily mindfulness, yoga, or meditation to center your thoughts and alleviate stress.

- Learning to pause and breathe can greatly help you regain focus in high-pressure situations. Even a few minutes a day can significantly impact your emotional well-being.

- Reflective Journaling: Document your journey by expressing your thoughts and feelings openly. This not only clarifies your mind but also helps you to identify patterns in your mindset and track progress over time.

- Visualization Techniques: Make a habit of visualizing your success. Imagining the realization of your goals can inspire and remind you of what you're working towards.

- Seek Feedback and Iterate: Seek constructive feedback from peers or mentors and use it to refine your approach. Iteration based on feedback is a powerful tool for improvement.

Emotional resilience doesn't mean being free from self-doubt or fear; rather, it involves knowing how to navigate these emotions and keep going despite them.

By adopting these practices, you prepare yourself for hurdles while building a strong foundation for your entrepreneurial journey.

Reflection Exercise:

Take a moment to jot down your biggest fears about starting your side hustle.

Next to each fear, write down one small step you can take to address it.

With a resilient mindset, you can now switch gears to focus on building a robust support network, a crucial next step in ensuring your venture remains on track and resilient against future challenges.

Building and Leveraging a Support Network

Entrepreneurship can be daunting, but you don't have to navigate it alone.

A strong support network can be your safety net, helping you to learn, grow, and push past challenges more effectively.

Establishing connections with mentors and engaging with communities of fellow entrepreneurs are crucial steps in building this network.

Finding Mentors

Mentors are invaluable, offering guidance based on their own experiences.

They can provide insights and advice that help you avoid common pitfalls and accelerate your growth.

Annette, for instance, found a mentor who had launched a similar online tutoring platform.

By sharing lessons from their own journey, the mentor helped Annette to refine her business model and navigate technical challenges more efficiently.

Engaging with Entrepreneurial Communities

Joining entrepreneurial communities, both online and offline, opens doors to sharing knowledge, resources, and experiences.

These platforms provide a space to brainstorm ideas, seek feedback, and find collaborators.

Emily found her breakthrough by actively participating in a local startup group, where she gleaned ideas and formed collaborations that enriched her business approach.

Peer Accountability Partnerships

A peer accountability partnership consists of regular check-ins with a fellow entrepreneur.

This relationship keeps you focused on your goals, provides encouragement, and offers fresh perspectives on your challenges.

When Annette partnered with an entrepreneur from a different industry, she gained valuable insights into time management and prioritization, which helped streamline her operations.

Building and nurturing a support network allows you to draw strength from the collective wisdom and encouragement of those around you.

This network fosters a sense of belonging and resilience, essential for navigating the ups and downs of entrepreneurship.

Building and nurturing a support network is crucial for any entrepreneur looking to overcome new challenges.

As we've seen, such connections provide not only practical advice but also the moral support that bolsters resilience.

With these networks in place, you're not only prepared to face obstacles, but you're also positioned to turn challenges into opportunities for growth.

Now, let's take a moment to reflect on how these experiences and connections shape a broader learning journey—an essential part of embracing the entrepreneurial learning curve.

CONCLUSION: EMBRACING THE LEARNING CURVE

Annette's journey is a great example of how resilience, adaptability, and strategic problem-solving can transform challenges into success.

Her story is a reminder that these same principles are within reach for anyone starting their entrepreneurial journey.

Each step, stumble, and triumph along your entrepreneurial journey is a part of the greater learning curve.

Embrace these moments with open arms, understanding that each challenge not only tests your resilience but also strengthens your adaptability and commitment to your vision.

Annette faced technical difficulties, marketing mishaps, and operational overload, yet it was her determination to learn from each experience that propelled her success.

Remember, resilience isn't just about bouncing back; it's about moving forward consistently, even when the path seems uncertain.

View every failure as an opportunity to gain insight—a chance to refine your approach and evolve into a more astute entrepreneur. This mindset will allow you to transform obstacles into valuable lessons that contribute to your ongoing development.

So, as you forge ahead, let these stories and strategies fortify your resolve. Face the entrepreneurial adventure with confidence, knowing you possess the tools to navigate through uncertainty and persist toward your aspirations.

ACTION EXERCISE:

Identify one challenge you're facing at this stage of your entrepreneurial journey.

List three possible solutions and choose one to implement this week.

Success depends on your ability to adapt, stay resilient, and continuously turn challenges into stepping stones for growth.

With these foundational strategies in place, you're ready to tackle the next vital aspect of your entrepreneurial journey: financing your passion project.

In the following chapter, we'll explore creative and strategic financial strategies necessary to support the thriving of your side hustle.

Get ready to unlock innovative solutions that will sustain and expand your venture's potential.

CHAPTER 8

FINANCING YOUR PASSION PROJECT

INTRODUCTION: JOHN'S FINANCING JOURNEY

Imagine the aroma of freshly baked croissants blending with the sounds of neighbors chatting in a sunlit bakery.

This was the dream that consumed John's thoughts.

John had spent years as a school principal.

Now in his 50s and surrounded by textbooks, he found himself daydreaming about buttery croissants and freshly brewed coffee.

He had a passion for artisanal baking.

It was more than a weekend hobby; it was a vision he yearned to share with the community through a quaint neighborhood bakery.

THE BEGINNING

Initially, John sought traditional financing methods: bank loans and personal savings.

However, he soon realized that traditional funding options were as rigid as a stale baguette.

Challenges mounted as rejection letters piled up, threatening to dampen his hopes.

THE PIVOT

John's breakthrough came when he discovered the potential of alternative financing.

He decided to embrace creativity, transforming the seemingly impossible into a thriving reality.

Crowdfunding platforms like Kickstarter became his financial launchpad.

With a compelling video showcasing his vision for community bonding over coffee and baked goods, John successfully appealed to those who shared his culinary enthusiasm.

While crowdfunding introduced John to supporters beyond his immediate reach, he quickly recognized that the roots of his dream lay even closer to home, in the relationships within his own neighborhood.

COMMUNITY SUPPORT

Beyond crowdfunding, John's greatest allies were right under his nose: the local community.

He organized local baking workshops and tastings, creating a buzz around his bakery.

These events not only showcased his talent but also turned supportive neighbors into investors, each contributing small amounts that collectively formed a significant base for his startup fund.

THE OUTCOME

By employing these resourceful strategies, John transformed not only his finances but his entire approach to entrepreneurship.

The bakery didn't just open—it flourished, becoming a thriving community hub.

John's journey highlights the transformative power of combining innovation with community spirit.

His innovative approach to overcoming financial challenges highlights the importance of thinking beyond traditional strategies.

As we move from his inspiring story into practical strategies, it's crucial to understand that every entrepreneurial success story begins with a solid financial plan.

It's not just about securing funds, but about aligning your passion with a sustainable business model.

In the following section, we'll explore the importance of identifying and understanding your financial needs—a pivotal step before exploring creative funding solutions.

By anticipating what you'll require financially while creating and building your new business, you'll be better equipped to tackle obstacles head-on and construct a resilient business that's designed for long-term success.

Let's begin this journey toward financial clarity and empowerment.

In this next section, we'll help you anticipate the financial requirements of your new venture, preparing you to tackle obstacles and build a resilient business from the ground up.

UNDERSTANDING YOUR FINANCIAL NEEDS

Starting a new business, whether it's the bakery of your dreams or another venture, requires more than passion—it demands a clear grasp of your financial landscape.

Success begins with identifying and mapping out your financial essentials.

INITIAL INVESTMENTS

Before diving into the excitement, take the time to pinpoint your startup costs.

For example, opening a bakery might require at least $5,000 for industrial ovens and $2,000 for initial ingredient stock.

Reflection Question:

Do you have what you need, financially, to start your own home-based online business?

List the top 3-5 things you'll need and how much you'll need to fund the items?

If you're starting a home-based online digital marketing business, you might need around $3,000+ for a computer, printer, and software, anywhere from $50 to $500 for a business license and permits, depending on your location, an average of $2,000+ for branding with a domain, website, logo, and hosting services, and marketing materials, such as business cards and digital graphics.

Does this align with your expectations?

Anything else you might need?

(Note: The items and costs will likely vary significantly depending on your business and its location, among other factors.)

It's crucial to account for the following key considerations:

- Equipment and Supplies: From ovens to spatulas, list every tool you'll need.

- Licensing and Permits: Research the legal requirements needed to operate in your specific location.

- Branding: Factor in design costs, website development, marketing materials, and other tools to create a cohesive identity.

Knowing these upfront prevents surprises and allows you to set realistic expectations.

These investments ensure your business is well-equipped, legally compliant, and ready to attract clients.

OPERATIONAL BUDGET

Once your business launches, it's essential to plan for the daily expenses that keep operations running smoothly:

- Rent, Mortgage, and Utilities: These fixed monthly costs should be prioritized in your budget.

- Inventory and Supplies: Regularly replenish your stock to meet customer demand.

- Marketing Efforts: From flyers to social media campaigns, allocate funds to reach and engage your audience.

Creating an operational budget helps you maintain steady growth without sacrificing quality or service.

BUILDING A FINANCIAL BUFFER

Unforeseen challenges are a part of life—and business is no exception.

This is where an emergency fund becomes invaluable.

Set aside a financial cushion for unforeseen hiccups—whether it's equipment repairs or market changes.

Building this safety net not only safeguards your venture, but also provides the peace of mind needed to focus on growth and innovation.

Understanding and organizing your finances isn't just about survival—it's about paving the way to a thriving, prosperous future.

A clear understanding of your financial landscape quips you to confidently navigate the challenges of entrepreneurship.

Now is the moment to think creatively and explore alternative funding paths that can unlock new opportunities.

By tapping into creative financial resources, you can overcome common obstacles and strengthen your resilience as you build your business.

EXPLORING CREATIVE FUNDING OPTIONS

When the traditional avenues close, it's time to get innovative.

As John discovered, using creative funding options can bridge the gap between dreams and reality.

Here are several paths that can help fund your venture:

Crowdfunding Platforms

As you saw with John's journey using Kickstarter, crowdfunding offers a unique opportunity to raise capital both locally and globally.

Through Kickstarter, John brought his vision of artisanal baking to a global audience, connecting with supporters who shared his passion.

The collective support not only provided the financial boost he needed, but also validated his business idea.

It fostered a sense of community around his bakery, offering a chance for a small business to grow exponentially by connecting the business with a worldwide network of supporters.

Another example of a professional who used crowdsourcing is Sarah, a retired teacher in her 60s.

Sarah used Kickstarter to fund her art studio, which she had dreamed about starting for years.

When people invested in her studio using Kickstarter, she offered her donors handmade art that she created in her studio.

This not only thanked her donors, but also introduced the donors to her art. As a result, not only did they continue to donate over the years, but they also became enthusiastic customers over the years.

The Pebble smartwatch campaign exemplifies how crowdfunding can transform a bold idea into a monumental success.

Developed by a team, eager to create a customizable watch that connected seamlessly with smartphones, Pebble turned to Kickstarter to fund their vision, appealing directly to enthusiasts with a shared interest.

Initially, they set a modest goal of $100,000. However, their campaign struck a chord with tech enthusiasts worldwide, ultimately raising over $10 million from tens of thousands of backers.

This overwhelming support not only provided the necessary funds but validated the market demand and established a dedicated customer base from the outset.

Here are a couple of important aspects when turning to Crowdfunding:

- Craft a Compelling Pitch: Share an authentic story and offer meaningful rewards to connect with potential backers.

- Engage Your Community: Use updates and social media to build lasting relationships and turn supporters into loyal advocates.

PERSONAL SAVINGS

Utilizing personal savings is often the first step.

While personal savings give you full control over your business, they demand disciplined budgeting to ensure financial security.

Set aside a specific portion of your savings dedicated solely to your business, ensuring you continue to live comfortably without compromising your financial security.

FRIENDS AND FAMILY

Tapping into your personal network can provide substantial support. Here's how to make it work effectively:

- Be Transparent: Share your business plan openly and specify the financial support you're seeking.

- Draft Formal Agreements: Clear, written terms protect relationships by preventing misunderstandings, even with close connections.

ANGEL INVESTORS

Angel investors provide more than just capital—they offer invaluable mentorship and access to expansive networks.

Consider Amazon, a prime example of a company that flourished with the support of early angel investors who provided critical funding and guidance.

In its infancy, Amazon was far from the e-commerce giant it is today.

Jeff Bezos, the founder, sought angel investors to get his online bookstore off the ground.

Key figures like Tom Alberg and Nick Hanauer saw potential in Bezos's vision and provided critical capital during Amazon's infancy.

More than just funding, these investors offered strategic advice, helping Bezos navigate the volatile landscape of online commerce.

Their support extended beyond financial backing, rooted in mentorship and a shared belief in Bezos's vision—a combination that proved crucial to Amazon's eventual success.

Key components of approaching Angel Investors:

- Understand Your Investor: Conduct thorough research to ensure their interests and expertise align with your business vision.

- Deliver a Detailed Pitch: Present a compelling, well-structured proposal that highlights your business's potential and unique value.

Angel Investors not only bring essential capital, but also offer strategic guidance and connect entrepreneurs with partners who can propel their businesses forward.

An example is that of the founders of Uber, Garrett Camp and Travis Kalanick.

They initially turned to angel investors for support, and found Chris Saca, an early investor who provided crucial funds, but also offered industry insights and connections that were invaluable in navigating regulatory challenges.

QUICK QUESTIONS:

We know that many startup entrepreneurs fund their new business using their own funds.

Where are your startup funds coming from?

Is it enough?

Grants and Competitions

Securing a grant or winning a competition can provide crucial funding and validate your business idea.

Programs like the Small Business Innovation Research (SBIR) grants support high-tech innovation without taking equity in your company.

When applying for grants or entering competitions, consider these key strategies to strengthen your approach:

- Align with Mission: Tailor applications to fit the mission and criteria of the granting organization.

- Preparation and Persistence: Be ready to invest time in preparation and learn from feedback to refine future applications.

Exploring these creative funding options can propel your business into its next phase of growth.

By being open to different sources and strategies, you maintain the flexibility to navigate financial challenges successfully.

With these creative funding avenues explored, you're well-positioned to fuel your business's early growth.

But securing funding is just one piece of the puzzle.

To truly thrive, you must manage your resources effectively.

In the next section, we'll explore how mastering cash flow management not only keeps your venture on track but also builds the resilience needed to tackle the inevitable bumps along the way.

Mastering Cash Flow Management

Managing cash flow effectively is crucial for ensuring your business's long-term success.

Here's how to maintain a healthy financial operation:

Diversify Revenue Streams:

- Minimize dependency on a single income source by diversifying your product and service offerings.

- Consider implementing subscription models to ensure stable income and forming strategic partnerships to reach new customers.

Manage Expenses:

- Reduce costs by automating routine tasks, negotiating favorable terms with suppliers, and outsourcing non-core activities to enhance efficiency.

Build Financial Resilience:

- Set aside a portion of your profits to establish emergency fund for unexpected expenses.

- Perform regular expense audits to uncover cost-saving opportunities and utilize cash flow projections to anticipate and plan for future financial needs.

Leverage Financial Tools:

- Use accounting software such as QuickBooks for real-time financial tracking, and integrate budgeting apps to streamline spending management.

ACTION EXERCISE:

Take five minutes to pinpoint a specific area where you could save or reallocate business funds, such as subscriptions, advertising expenses, or freelancers usage.

Which cash flow management principles would you apply?

By adopting these strategies, you can avoid financial strain and pave the way for sustainable growth.

Mastering cash flow ensures your business can adapt to changing markets and continue to thrive with steady economic management.

In today's dynamic marketplace, adopting the right financial tools and technologies can streamline operations and enhance strategic decision-making.

These innovations are essential for overcoming obstacles and driving your venture towards sustained success.

ie right tools can revolutionize business
...ifying complex tasks and freeing up time
owth.

...ook at some essential technologies that every
small business can benefit from:

ACCOUNTING SOFTWARE: QUICKBOOKS

Effective financial management is crucial for business success, and using the right accounting software can greatly aid this process:

QuickBooks:

- QuickBooks offers an intuitive platform for managing business finances, enabling you to track income, expenses, and sales with ease.

- It provides instant insights through easy-to-read dashboards, simplifies tax preparation, and keeps financial records organized, reducing the risk of errors while saving time.

Xero:

- Known for its robust features and seamless integration with other business tools, Xero offers detailed reports, expense claims, and inventory tracking.

- Its user-friendly interface and cloud-based access make it a strong choice for businesses that value flexibility and collaboration.

FreshBooks:

- Ideal for service-based businesses, FreshBooks excels in invoicing and time-tracking.

- FreshBooks streamlines billing with features to manage recurring invoices and track billable hours efficiently.

- Its straightforward interface and excellent customer support make accounting less daunting for small business owners.

These accounting software options provide comprehensive tools tailored to various business needs.

This ensures that you can manage your finances efficiently and focus on strategic growth.

ONLINE PAYMENT PLATFORMS

To thrive in today's competitive business landscape, businesses must cater to diverse customer payment preferences.

Here's how various platforms can enhance your transaction processes:

PayPal:

- A widely trusted platform, PayPal provides robust security and instant transfers to business accounts, streamlining cash flow management.

- Seamlessly integrating with e-commerce platforms, PayPal enables businesses to reach a global audience while facilitating secure and convenient online transactions.

Stripe:

- Renowned for its developer-friendly API, Stripe supports both online and in-person transactions, offering unparalleled versatility for businesses.

- This makes Stripe versatile for businesses of all sizes.

- Stripe's detailed analytics and subscription billing options empower businesses to customize payment solutions, ensuring ease of use and scalability.

By incorporating these payment platforms, businesses can address diverse customer preferences, ensuring seamless and efficient transactions.

Embracing digital payment solutions enables businesses to reach a wider audience while elevating the overall customer experience.

This approach fosters customer loyalty and drives sales, contributing to sustained business growth and stability.

BUDGETING APPS:

Managing business finances becomes simpler and more effective with the use of budgeting apps:

Mint:

- Designed for entrepreneurs, Mint offers a comprehensive view of spending and effortless budget-setting capabilities.

- By aggregating financial data, it helps users identify trends and make informed, goal-aligned decisions.

YNAB (You Need A Budget):

- YNAB emphasizes proactive budgeting, guiding businesses to assign every dollar a purpose while dynamically adjusting budgets as needed.

- Ideal for those wanting precise control over their finances, YNAB helps ensure that your cash flow aligns with your goals.

PocketGuard:

- Celebrated for its simplicity, PocketGuard efficiently tracks spending and manages budgets.

- With real-time updates on available funds after accounting for bills and necessities, it's ideal for entrepreneurs seeking straightforward financial oversight.

Goodbudget:

- Goodbudget employs the envelope budgeting method, enabling businesses to allocate funds across categories and foster disciplined spending habits.

- This method enhances cash flow management and supports financial stability.

These budgeting apps offer a range of features that cater to different financial management styles, empowering businesses to maintain financial health and make strategic planning decisions with confidence.

BLOCKCHAIN FOR TRANSPARENCY

Although still an emerging technology, blockchain creates secure records that can't be altered.

By providing tamper-proof records, blockchain helps businesses build trust with partners and customers while reducing the risk of fraud and disputes.

Integrating these tools enhances the efficiency and accuracy of financial management, establishing a strong foundation for sustainable business growth.

Embracing technology isn't just about keeping up; it's about setting up your enterprise for success in a competitive landscape.

Equipped with the right tools and technologies, businesses can efficiently manage finances.

However, building a resilient financial strategy remains vital to safeguarding against unforeseen challenges.

Let's explore how you can anticipate obstacles and develop robust problem-solving strategies to ensure your venture remains secure and thriving.

BUILDING FINANCIAL RESILIENCE

Embarking on the entrepreneurial journey is both an emotional and financial endeavor.

For many professionals over 50, the prospect of starting from scratch can be daunting.

Entrepreneurs frequently encounter emotional challenges such as the fear of rejection and uncertainty about securing funding.

These feelings are natural but manageable with the right mindset and strategies.

It's never too late to transform your experience into success.

FACING EMOTIONAL CHALLENGES

Acknowledging the fear of rejection or anxiety about financial uncertainty is the first step toward overcoming these challenges.

Remember, every rejection is not an endpoint, but rather a stepping stone that sharpens your approach and strengthens your resilience.

TIPS FOR EMOTIONAL RESILIENCE:

- Stay Grounded in Your Vision: Maintain focus on your ultimate goal and use it as motivation to overcome obstacles.

- Learn from Setbacks: Treat every setback as an opportunity to learn and refine your strategy.

- Seek Support: Cultivate a network of mentors or fellow entrepreneurs to gain guidance and reduce feelings of isolation.

RISK MANAGEMENT

A strategic approach to identifying potential risks can help mitigate their impact.

Whether it's economic shifts or unexpected operational challenges, having contingency plans in place ensures your business can weather the storms.

KEY RISK MANAGEMENT STRATEGIES:

- Conduct Regular Assessments: Regularly assess internal and external factors that could impact your business.

- Diversify Income Streams: Diversifying income streams reduces reliance on a single source and cushions against market fluctuations.

FINANCIAL BUFFERS

Establishing a financial buffer is essential for maintaining stability during economic fluctuations or unexpected expenses.

Strive to save enough funds to cover at least three to six months of expenses, creating a safety net during lean periods.

DEBT MANAGEMENT

Effective debt management prevents it from becoming a growth-stifling burden.

Prioritize paying off high-interest debts and consider refinancing for better terms to improve liquidity.

DEBT MANAGEMENT TIPS:

- Communicate with Creditors: Maintaining open communication with creditors can lead to more favorable repayment terms.

- Stay Disciplined: Consistently review and adhere to repayment plans to ensure debts are managed promptly.

Financial resilience involves equipping yourself with the tools to address both emotional and financial challenges effectively.

Remember that it's the ability to adapt and innovate that truly sets successful ventures apart.

By cultivating a resilient mindset and implementing strategic financial practices, you create a venture that not only survives, but thrives, unlocking future opportunities.

Reflection Question:

Have you identified someone who can provide emotional support during your business startup?

Have you prepared a backup plan or financial buffer to address unforeseen financial challenges?

Let's wrap up this chapter by reinforcing how these elements come together to fuel sustainable growth and long-term success.

Conclusion: Financing for Sustainable Growth

Embarking on the entrepreneurial journey is an adventure driven by passion, creativity, and determination.

Every successful business is built on a foundation of resilience and strategic financial planning.

As discussed in this chapter, financing your passion project offers numerous opportunities for innovation and adaptation.

Key Takeaways:

Embrace Creativity in Financing:

- Break free from conventional funding paths by exploring diverse sources such as crowdfunding, angel investors, or alternative financing methods.

Understand Your Financial Needs:

- Start with a clear understanding of your initial costs and ongoing obligations to build a strong foundation for success.

Master Cash Flow and Harness Tools:

- Utilize financial tools and strategies to maintain organization and foster growth.

Build Financial Resilience:

- Tackle emotional and practical challenges with confidence by employing effective risk management and debt strategies.

Adaptability, innovation, and strategic planning form the cornerstones of sustainable growth.

Let these principles guide you to not only survive, but thrive.

Every challenge offers an opportunity to refine your vision, and every success serves as a launchpad to greater achievements.

Your passion project is not just a dream—it's your legacy.

With a solid plan and a willingness to adapt, your venture will reach new heights and lay the foundation for long-term triumph.

ACTION EXERCISE:

Take the next step by assessing your financial needs and exploring creative options that align with your vision.

Begin by mapping out your startup costs and creating a detailed list of the anticipated initial expenses.

This exercise will help you set realistic financial expectations and avoid unexpected challenges.

Remember, the most successful entrepreneurs are not those who faced no obstacles, but those who turned challenges into stepping stones to success.

As you establish a solid financial foundation, your business will be poised to soar beyond its starting point.

In the next chapter, we will explore strategies to expand your reach and diversify your offerings, transforming potential growth into measurable success.

CHAPTER 9

GROWING BEYOND THE INITIAL LAUNCH

INTRODUCTION: THE UNFOLDING PATHS OF SARAH AND JOY

Sarah's journey began with a deep-seated passion for crafting candles, each one uniquely imbued with a story, a captivating aroma, and a distinct aesthetic.

Imagine Sarah at her kitchen table, surrounded by wax and wicks, meticulously crafting candles that illuminated rooms while igniting imaginations.

The thrill of launching her online store was immediate, as orders poured in and her inbox brimmed with enthusiastic messages.

Yet, as the novelty wore off, so did the momentum. Sales plateaued, leaving her business at risk of stagnation.

Refusing to let her passion dim, Sarah faced this challenge head-on with determination and creativity.

She realized that the solution lay not just in making more candles but in telling their stories to a wider audience.

Leveraging digital marketing and connecting directly with her community through storytelling and interactive social media, she reignited interest and expanded her brand beyond its early beginnings.

Her journey is a testament to resilience—moving beyond mere survival to thrive.

Like Sarah, Joy Mangano's journey was defined by tenacity and a flair for innovation.

Known for the revolutionary Miracle Mop, Joy's path was far from seamless.

Even with a groundbreaking product like the Miracle Mop, Joy faced rejection from traditional retail channels. But Joy, with her inventive spirit, turned hurdles into stepping stones.

She saw beyond the constraints of conventional sales channels and embraced digital platforms wholeheartedly.

Infomercials became the cornerstone of her success, enabling her to connect with audiences through authentic storytelling and a compelling vision.

Joy's transformation from an innovator frustrated by limitations to a household name illuminates the power of resourcefulness.

Her choice to narrate her own story amplified her reach, proving that authenticity and a direct connection with the customer can turn dreams into reality.

Together, these stories illustrate that at the heart of entrepreneurship lies not just the spark of an idea, but the relentless drive to keep it alive and growing.

We also see how crucial it can be to adopt innovative strategies and leverage new technologies.

These approaches not only optimize daily operations but also expand market reach, build brand resilience, and foster sustainable business growth.

Sarah and Joy's journeys show that while passion ignites the initial spark, overcoming growth challenges requires thoughtful strategies and a willingness to adapt.

Let's explore key strategies that can help you navigate these challenges and guide you through the growth phases of your new business journey.

STRATEGIES FOR SCALING OPERATIONS

Scaling a business is like climbing a mountain—a journey that demands preparation, resilience, and deliberate strategy.

Let's explore some key strategies that can help you ascend to new heights while overcoming common barriers.

AUTOMATION AND SYSTEMATIZATION

When your business starts to grow, keeping the quality consistent can be challenging.

Automation streamlines repetitive tasks, reduces errors, and frees up your team to focus on higher value work.

For instance, automating customer service replies can save significant time and effort.

Doing this not only makes your operations more efficient but also helps ensure your products or services are consistently delivered with high quality.

ACTIONABLE SOLUTIONS:

- Start Small: Use tools like Zapier for automating workflows or Trello for efficient project management.

- Invest in Technology: Use platforms like HubSpot for marketing automation.

- Continuous Review: Regularly assess tools like Google Analytics to improve automated processes.

Consider 'Sweet Crumbs,' a successful online bakery operated by a couple in their 50s.

They founded the bakery as a small, family-run business with the aim of sharing their passion for baked goods with their community.

However, as demand grew, they began receiving more orders, including requests for deliveries outside their local area. They struggled to keep up with the growing demand.

They feared the quality of their baked goods might suffer due to the increased order volume.

To address this, they turned to tools like Zapier and Trello to streamline order management.

Orders placed through Shopify were automatically organized and tracked, which streamlined the process and improved efficiency. Through automation and streamlined processes, they successfully scaled their business while maintaining high service and product quality.

They allowed them to focus on crafting new flavors and strengthening customer relationships.

Reflective Questions:

Reflect on your business today: What challenges are you encountering as it grows, and how can automation tools help address these?

Which strategy fits your needs right now, and what's one step you can take this week to put it into action?

Now, before looking for outside tools to improve your processes, it's important to first look inward to capitalize on what you're already doing well.

LEVERAGING EXISTING SUCCESS

Remember, you have already experienced successes. It's important to acknowledge these achievements and explore ways to leverage them.

Identify your top-performing products or services and amplify their reach through targeted marketing and promotional efforts.

ACTIONABLE SOLUTIONS:

- Analyze Data: Use tools like Google Data Studio or Tableau to gain visual insights into performance.

- Expand Marketing Efforts: Leverage Hootsuite or Buffer for social media marketing extensions.

- Optimize Channels: Use A/B testing on platforms like Optimizely to determine effective channels.

MARKET EXPANSION

Expanding into new markets can help you reach more customers and drive business growth.

To do this successfully, you need to plan carefully and understand the new area.

This means looking at who your potential customers are, being aware of cultural differences, and knowing the rules and regulations you must follow.

By taking these steps, you can lay the groundwork for successful growth in new markets.

ACTIONABLE SOLUTIONS:

- Research Thoroughly: Utilize market research tools like Euromonitor or Nielsen.

- Start Locally: Use platforms like Shopify to test ecommerce strategies domestically.

- Adapt Strategies: Employ Geo-targeting with Google Ads to cater to local preferences.

PARTNERSHIPS AND COLLABORATIONS

Scaling your business doesn't have to be a solo journey.

Strategic partnerships can unlock new audiences and resources.

Partnering with complementary businesses can yield mutually beneficial outcomes.

ACTIONABLE SOLUTIONS:

- Identify Strategic Partners: Leverage community groups or business networking sites such as LinkedIn or Indeed to find potential partners.

- Joint Ventures: Platforms like Kickstarter can be used for collaborative project funding.

- Share Success: Use software like Slack for seamless collaboration and communication.

FRANCHISING AND LICENSING

For some businesses, franchising or licensing offer a strategic way to scale rapidly without the significant investment typically required for opening new locations or markets.

It enables you to expand your brand's reach by utilizing franchisees' capital.

Actionable Solutions:

- Standardize Operations: Use resources like Franchise Direct to learn about creating operations manuals.

- Select the Right Franchisees: Platforms like Franchise Gator can help find qualified individuals.

- Provide Ongoing Support: Consider using Learning Management Systems (LMS) like Litmos for training.

Scaling your business presents challenges, particularly in managing quality, maintaining cash flow, and adapting to new markets.

However, by implementing these strategies thoughtfully, you can transform these challenges into stepping stones toward sustained growth and success.

Once effective scaling strategies are in place, the next frontier is diversifying your offerings.

This approach not only broadens your market appeal but also leverages innovative strategies and technologies to enhance brand resilience and drive sustainable growth.

Building upon the essential strategies for scaling operations, let's examine how Apple Inc. exemplifies strategic diversification, offering key lessons on how to expand market presence by fostering innovation.

Case Study: Apple Inc.

Apple's strategic diversification provides an exemplary case of effective market expansion.

Originally known for personal computers, Apple successfully expanded into the mobile and wearable tech industries, with products like the iPod, iPhone, iPad, and Apple Watch.

The company's diversification strategy is heavily driven by customer feedback and pilot launches.

Each new product sees a small initial release, with feedback rigorously analyzed before full market introduction.

This approach has allowed Apple to incrementally refine their offerings and maintain their reputation as an innovator in technology, leading to expanding and diversifying their product lines.

This naturally leads us to explore how expanding your own product and service offerings can bolster resilience and extend market reach.

This strategy helps a business address evolving customer needs in an increasingly competitive market landscape.

PRODUCT AND SERVICE DIVERSIFICATION

Expanding your product or service offerings can boost your business's resilience and extend its market reach.

By introducing new products or services, you unlock the potential to meet evolving customer needs and stand out in a crowded marketplace.

Now, let's explore the key components of successful diversification.

Assessing Opportunities

Before venturing into new product lines, it's crucial to assess where opportunities lie.

This involves understanding market trends, identifying gaps in your offerings, and forecasting future demand.

Tools like SWOT analysis and market research reports can be invaluable in this process, helping to pinpoint where your business can naturally extend its offerings.

Reflection Exercise

Reflect on your current product or service.

What untapped customer needs could you address through new offerings?

Consider what complementary products or services could enhance your existing lineup, fostering greater customer satisfaction and loyalty.

CUSTOMER FEEDBACK

Listening to your customers is one of the simplest yet most powerful ways to guide diversification.

Customer feedback offers direct insights into your market, uncovering unmet needs, desires, and opportunities for innovation.

Surveys, focus groups, and social media interactions are all valuable channels for gathering feedback.

By engaging with your audience, you not only discover what they want but build loyalty through involvement in your brand's evolution.

PILOT LAUNCHES

Testing new offerings in a controlled, smaller-scale environment minimizes risk and provides valuable insights.

A pilot launch enables you to gather data on customer reactions, refine your product through real-world use, and prepare for a wider rollout.

This strategy ensures that any necessary tweaks are identified and addressed before full-scale production.

Example: A Bakery Adding Cooking Classes

Consider Jean Smith, a seasoned entrepreneur in her fifties who owned a thriving bakery.

Renowned for her artisan bread, Jean saw an opportunity to diversify by offering cooking classes.

Recognizing a growing interest in home baking, she launched a series of workshops that quickly gained popularity.

Jean's approach was simple yet effective: she leveraged her existing expertise and client base to introduce a service that complemented her products.

This diversification not only boosted her revenue, but also strengthened her brand's reputation as a community hub for learning and high-quality food.

COMPLEMENTARY OFFERINGS

The introduction of complementary products can enhance the customer experience and add value to your primary offerings.

For instance, if you sell fitness equipment, offering a related app to track workouts can add significant value.

This strategy can help in upselling by providing customers with a more comprehensive solution that meets multiple needs.

Diversifying your products and services helps build a more robust and adaptable business model.

By assessing opportunities, listening intently to customer feedback, and conducting pilot launches, you can ensure that each new venture strengthens your brand's foundation.

After diversifying your offerings, the next essential step is harnessing the power of technology and AI.

These tools are crucial not just for optimizing operations but also for expanding market reach and building a resilient brand capable of sustainable growth.

Let's discover how you can leverage these technologies to propel your business forward.

Leveraging Technology and AI

As businesses evolve, strategically leveraging technology and AI can enhance operations and customer experiences.

Let's explore how these innovations shape the e-commerce landscape and optimize supply chains using data-driven approaches.

Potential Challenges and Mitigation Strategies

Integrating new technology presents challenges, including upfront costs and a steep learning curve, which can be daunting for many businesses.

However, by selecting scalable, intuitive solutions, businesses can ease the transition and spread initial costs over time.

Training is crucial—equipping your team with the skills to effectively use these technologies minimizes disruptions.

Moreover, collaborating with tech vendors who offer comprehensive support ensures a smoother implementation process.

By tackling these hurdles head-on, your business can fully harness the potential of technological advancements, laying the foundation for sustainable growth.

Once the groundwork is laid through strategic tech integration and strong vendor partnerships, businesses are primed to capitalize on groundbreaking e-commerce innovations.

These innovations can further enhance customer experiences and satisfaction while driving sales.

E-Commerce Innovations

In e-commerce, technologies like Augmented Reality (AR) and Artificial Intelligence (AI) are transforming customer experiences.

For example, IKEA uses AR in its app, allowing customers to virtually place furniture in their homes before buying.

This innovation has increased customer engagement, reducing return rates and boosting sales.

Sephora also uses AI to enhance personalization.

Their virtual artist app uses AR to enable customers to try on makeup via their smartphones, leading to higher customer satisfaction and increased conversion rates.

AI's ability to personalize experiences is measurable, with Sephora reporting significant growth in app engagement and product sales.

STREAMLINING SUPPLY CHAINS

Modern supply chains are increasingly integrated with technology to improve efficiency and visibility.

The Internet of Things (IoT) and blockchain technology are revolutionizing supply chain management by improving transparency, efficiency, and accountability.

In industries where product quality and compliance are critical, blockchain technology has become a game-changer.

Companies such as Walmart are using blockchain to ensure transparency in their supply chains.

And in 2021, according to Statistica, approximately 29% of small to medium-sized businesses were using blockchain technology.

By creating a digital ledger that records every transaction and movement of goods, blockchain enables stakeholders to trace product origins and verify authenticity at each stage.

This capability is essential in sectors such as food and pharmaceuticals, where product recalls can be costly and damage reputations. The transparency provided by blockchain technology not only builds trust with consumers but also streamlines regulatory compliance processes.

IoT devices significantly improve inventory management and logistics by providing real-time data visibility.

For instance, Amazon uses IoT technology in its warehouses to monitor goods in transit and optimize their logistics operations.

Sensors track the movement of packages and relay information on location, temperature, and handling conditions, which ensures items are delivered efficiently and in optimal condition.

This real-time data enables businesses to react swiftly to potential issues, minimizing delays and reducing operational costs.

By implementing IoT solutions, companies can improve their operational efficiency, reduce waste, and enhance customer satisfaction through faster and more reliable deliveries.

Together, IoT and blockchain empower businesses with the tools needed to maintain competitive delivery standards in an ever-evolving market landscape.

REAL-WORLD EXAMPLE: JOHN DEERE

John Deere, a global leader in agricultural machinery, is setting the standard for innovation by incorporating IoT technology into its operations.

This advancement turns traditional farming into a high-tech, data-driven process.

By equipping their equipment with IoT sensors, John Deere provides farmers with real-time insights into everything from soil conditions to equipment performance. Imagine being able to optimize your harvest with precise knowledge of when and where to plant, water, or harvest.

This level of insight transforms farming efficiency and productivity, directly affecting the bottom line for farmers. They can now make data-informed decisions that maximize crop yields while minimizing resource use.

For a farmer, this doesn't just mean enhanced operational efficiency—it signifies a revolution in how farming is approached, paving the way for sustainable agriculture.

For the business, this technology boosts product reliability and strengthens customer satisfaction.

Farmers become more than just equipment users; they become partners in innovation, part of a forward-thinking community that values progress and efficiency.

John Deere's use of modern technology highlights the transformative power of IoT in traditional industries, encouraging others to consider how embracing new technologies can drive significant improvements.

Regardless of your industry—whether technology, agriculture, or beyond—embracing innovation drives your business forward and creates a meaningful impact on the world.

DATA-DRIVEN APPROACHES

Utilizing data analytics allows businesses to make informed decisions based on substantial insights into consumer behavior and market trends.

Companies like Netflix leverage predictive analytics to personalize content recommendations, leading to increased viewer engagement and retention.

Adopting these technologies not only optimizes daily operations but also builds resilience against market fluctuations.

By embracing data-driven strategies, businesses can ensure sustained growth and a competitive edge.

As technology and AI pave the way for efficiency and improved customer interactions, the next logical progression is to develop a sustainable business model.

This ensures the technologies and strategies you've embraced translate into enduring success and resilience, positioning your business to thrive in an ever-changing market landscape.

Let's explore how a sustainable model anchors your growth and innovation.

Building a Sustainable Business Model

Building a sustainable business model lays the groundwork for long-term success.

It's not just about surviving today—it's about thriving tomorrow and leaving a legacy of innovation and responsibility. Here are the key elements that drive sustainability in business.

MISSION ALIGNMENT

At the heart of any successful business is a clear and aligned mission.

Your mission serves as the compass, guiding every decision and action.

It fuels passion, aligns team efforts, and fosters loyalty among your customers.

When your mission resonates with both your team and your market, it transcends the scope of day-to-day operations, ensuring every strategy is rooted in shared goals.

ACTIONABLE STEPS:

- Clarify Your Purpose: Ensure that everyone in your organization understands and supports the mission.

- Engage Employees: Regularly communicate how their roles align with the mission, fostering a sense of purpose and commitment.

- Reflect Values in Products: Ensure that your offerings consistently reflect the core values driving your mission.

RESOURCE MANAGEMENT

Effective resource management involves maximizing current assets while strategically planning for future growth.

By managing your staff and finances wisely, you can improve your business operations, boost productivity, and grow without compromising the quality of your products or services.

Embracing technology to simplify tasks can make this process even more efficient, helping you get the best results from your efforts.

ACTIONABLE STEPS:

- Implement Efficient Systems: Utilize software that enhances productivity and reduces waste, like Enterprise Resource Planning (ERP) systems.

- Invest in Training: Continuously develop your team's skills through ongoing education and targeted training programs to help them adapt and maximize the potential of new technologies.

- Financial Prudence: Ensure financial decisions align with long-term sustainability goals, balancing immediate needs with future investment.

ENVIRONMENTAL AND SOCIAL CONSIDERATIONS

Today's market demands more than just profitability—it calls for responsibility.

Companies that integrate environmental and social considerations into their business model contribute to a better world while building brand loyalty and resilience.

Consumers are increasingly drawn to brands that reflect their values, giving those that lead in sustainable practices a competitive edge.

ACTIONABLE STEPS:

- Adopt Sustainable Practices: Minimize waste, prioritize renewable resources, and reduce your environmental footprint.

- Community Engagement: Actively participate in social initiatives that align with your mission, furthering your commitment to societal well-being.

- Transparency and Accountability: Communicate openly about your sustainability efforts and achievements to build trust with consumers.

By embedding these elements into your business model, you not only ensure operational excellence but also align your enterprise with broader societal goals.

This approach not only strengthens your brand's resilience and reach but also fosters long-term growth and a positive environmental impact.

With a sustainable business model in place, you're poised to embrace innovation and growth.

Yet, as with any growth journey comes, challenges are inevitable.

Recognizing these challenges and implementing strategies to overcome them is critical for optimizing operations, expanding market reach, and building a resilient brand that stands the test of time.

Let's explore how to tackle these challenges effectively.

OVERCOMING CHALLENGES

Scaling a business is an exhilarating journey, but it's not without its hurdles.

Just as Sarah and Joy discovered, recognizing these common challenges early on can make all the difference in transforming potential roadblocks into gateways for growth.

OPERATIONAL INEFFICIENCIES

As Sarah scaled her candle business, she quickly realized that processes effective in small-scale production became cumbersome with increased demand.

She faced bottlenecks that slowed down her once-efficient operations.

STRATEGIES TO ADDRESS:

- Streamline Processes: Sarah adopted workflow management tools like Trello to track and streamline production tasks, helping her team stay organized and efficient.

- Adopt Automation: By automating inventory management, Sarah freed up her team to focus on creativity rather than logistics.

- Regular Audits: Conducting regular operational audits helped Sarah identify inefficiencies and continuously refine her processes.

CULTURAL MISALIGNMENT

Joy's expansion into digital marketing introduced new team members and perspectives, challenging her to preserve the core values that define her brand.

STRATEGIES TO ADDRESS:

- Communicate Values Clearly: Like Joy, regularly reinforcing the mission and values across all levels of your organization helps maintain a consistent culture even as the team grows.

- Foster Inclusivity: Joy encouraged an environment where diverse voices and ideas were welcomed, keeping her innovative spirit alive.

- Leadership Training: Equipping her team leads to manage change effectively, Joy ensured alignment with the company's core values even when expanding rapidly.

COMMON PITFALLS

Both Sarah and Joy faced challenges, such as meeting demand and maintaining quality, which taught them the value of preparation.

PRACTICAL SOLUTIONS:

- Scalable Systems: Ensure your systems for communication, accounting, and other essential functions can scale with growing demands.

- Financial Management: Maintain a solid financial plan to support growth without overextending resources.

- Customer Clarity: Prioritize customer needs and feedback to ensure that your scaling efforts meet or exceed their expectations.

By addressing these challenges proactively, you pave the way for smoother, more sustainable growth.

Like Sarah and Joy, it's about not only anticipating potential issues but equipping yourself with the tools and strategies to overcome them effectively.

Having navigated the complexities of scaling and overcoming its inherent challenges, your journey toward optimizing operations and expanding market reach now reaches a pivotal moment.

In the conclusion, we will bring together the key insights and strategies, reinforcing how innovation and resilience create a sustainable and thriving business foundation.

CONCLUSION: INNOVATING TODAY FOR A THRIVING TOMORROW

Reflecting on this chapter's insights, the path to sustainable success clearly hinges on innovation and resilience.

The journeys of Sarah and Joy highlight how adapting to change and leveraging modern technologies can optimize operations and expand market reach.

Their experiences show that combining strategic planning with a drive for innovation can lead to significant business growth.

The future of your business hinges on your ability to be agile and responsive.

By continuously aligning your mission with your strategies and embracing the advancements in technology, you can turn challenges into opportunities for growth.

To guide your journey forward, here's a concise summary of key takeaways—reinforcing the message that overcoming challenges leads to lasting success:

KEY STRATEGIES AND TAKEAWAYS:

- Adopt Automation and Systematization:
    - Use technology to streamline processes, boosting efficiency and quality.
    - Sarah's story illustrates how automation can stabilize operations while fostering creative focus.
- Leverage Existing Success:
    - Leverage your existing strengths to fuel growth.
    - Joy's experience demonstrates how amplifying what works best can expand market presence.
- Expand Your Market Reach:

- Approach new markets strategically, equipped for audience and operational challenges.
- Both Sarah and Joy demonstrated the potential of expanding beyond conventional boundaries.
- Foster Strategic Partnerships:
  - Collaborate with complementary businesses to broaden resources and market impact.
  - Joy accomplished this through building strategic alliances.
- Diversify with Intent:
  - Introduce new products or services that align with your brand and respond to customer needs and desires, as Sarah's unique candle offerings showed.
- Utilize Technology and Data:
  - Use AI, IoT, and other digital tools to improve decision-making and operational resilience, as demonstrated by both Sarah and Joy.
- Build a Sustainable Model:
  - Incorporate environmental and social principles to cultivate trust and resilience.
  - Both Sarah and Joy demonstrated how aligning with broader social values facilitates sustainable growth.

Remember, the landscape of business is ever-changing, but with a commitment to innovation and resilience, your venture can not only survive but thrive.

Let adaptability guide your strategies and decisions, securing long-term success and a lasting impact.

Just as Sarah rekindled her candle business and Joy revolutionized household products, you too can build a venture that thrives on innovation and resilience.

Don't wait—start transforming your business vision into reality today.

Start today by taking that first small step towards innovation. Whether it's automating a task, exploring a new market, or simply redefining your mission, the journey to success begins with a decisive action.

Trust in your experience, embrace the opportunities, and watch your business thrive just as Sarah and Joy did.

Now is your time to lead with courage and creativity!

With your business now poised for growth, the next focus is on developing the mindset that drives sustained success.

Chapter 10 delves into the critical role of continuous learning and adaptability in fostering an entrepreneurial mindset—equipping you to thrive in today's ever-evolving business landscape.

CHAPTER 10

CULTIVATING AN ENTREPRENEURIAL MINDSET

INTRODUCTION: AWAKENING THE ENTREPRENEURIAL SPIRIT

Meet Steve, an engineer whose predictable life took a transformative turn, awakening his entrepreneurial spirit.

Steve excelled as an engineer, where problem-solving came naturally.

But nearing his fifties, he faced a growing stagnation as the work that once inspired him became repetitive, leaving his creativity untapped and ambitions unfulfilled.

Steve found himself standing at a crossroads: to remain in the safety of familiarity or to forge a new path that resonated with his evolving passions.

Steve's awakening came unexpectedly, sparked by a simple realization: his talent for tinkering with tools and gadgets could evolve into a thriving tech consultancy.

This marked the beginning of a journey filled with uncertainties but also unparalleled opportunities for growth.

Embracing an entrepreneurial mindset became his guiding principle, rooted in the commitment to continual learning and adaptability.

By viewing failures as stepping stones and challenges as catalysts for innovation, Steve redefined both his career and his approach to life.

His transformation into an entrepreneur wasn't just about business—it was about applying adaptability and creativity to every facet of life.

It was through this shift in mindset that Steve realized true success doesn't merely stem from groundbreaking ideas but thrives through cultivating a mindset open to change and lifelong learning.

Steve's journey demonstrates how an entrepreneurial mindset—rooted in adaptability, creativity, and resilience—is key to navigating today's ever-changing market landscape.

This is particularly crucial for those embarking on their entrepreneurial path later in life.

Steve's story vividly illuminates how a steadfast commitment to this mindset unlocks boundless potential and enriches both our personal and professional lives.

Building on Steve's story, let's now explore the foundation of the entrepreneurial mindset—adaptability, creativity, and resilience—and how these traits foster a thriving entrepreneurial spirit.

THE FOUNDATION: WHAT IS AN ENTREPRENEURIAL MINDSET?

The entrepreneurial mindset—an essential foundation for any successful business—is a dynamic blend of adaptability, resilience, and creativity.

While these concepts have been introduced, let's now examine the key features of the entrepreneurial mindset more closely.

It's not merely about launching a new product or service; It's about adopting a way of thinking that embraces change, seeks innovation, allows an opportunity to rediscover your passions and create meaningful change, thriving even when the future seems uncertain.

Case Study: Eleanor Davies and "Evolving Strategies"

In her early fifties, Eleanor Davies of Santa Barbara, California, transformed her extensive expertise in traditional marketing into a thriving digital marketing agency.

She founded her own agency called "Evolving Strategies."

Overcoming age-based stereotypes and biases, Eleanor demonstrated her adaptability and showcased innovation that's crucial for entrepreneurship by mastering digital trends like SEO and social media marketing.

Her deep understanding of consumer behavior, drawn from years in the corporate sector, enabled her to offer unique insights that translated into tangible business solutions.

Eleanor's dedication to fostering a collaborative team—bringing together young tech enthusiasts and seasoned marketers—not only bridged generational gaps, but also highlighted the value of diverse perspectives.

Her story illustrates how adapting an entrepreneurial mindset—overcoming age biases, prioritizing measurable results, embracing adaptability, and building strong relationships—can drive success in the ever-evolving business landscape and inspire professionals over 50 to pursue new ventures with confidence.

ADAPTABILITY: THE POWER OF FLEXIBILITY

Adaptability is the ability to pivot and recalibrate in response to the unpredictable nature of business.

It involves being open to change and ready to recalibrate strategies as circumstances evolve.

In a world where market dynamics and consumer preferences are ever-changing, adaptability allows entrepreneurs to stay relevant and competitive.

For instance, during economic shifts or technological advancements, those who adapt quickly can turn potential threats into opportunities for growth.

By embracing adaptability, entrepreneurs position themselves to tackle uncertainty and leverage it as a strategic advantage.

RESILIENCE: RISING FROM SETBACKS

According to Oxford Languages, resilience is "the capacity to <u>withstand</u> or recover quickly from difficulties; <u>toughness</u>."

It's the grit that keeps entrepreneurs moving forward in the face of challenges.

Being resilient doesn't mean never experiencing failure; it means viewing setbacks as stepping stones rather than stumbling blocks.

Entrepreneurs with resilience are often those who, like Steve, learn from their failures, refine their strategies, and keep pushing towards their goals with renewed vigor.

This quality ensures sustained progress, even when the journey gets tough.

CREATIVITY: FUEL FOR INNOVATION

Creativity ignites innovation, serving as the driving force behind fresh ideas and solutions.

An entrepreneurial mindset taps into creative thinking to solve problems uniquely and explore new possibilities.

Creative entrepreneurs look beyond traditional solutions, often blending insights from diverse disciplines to craft novel approaches.

This mindset not only leads to the development of breakthrough products or services but also inspires a culture of continuous improvement and ingenuity within the organization.

Together, these three elements form the foundation of an entrepreneurial mindset, setting the stage for building a successful, sustainable business.

It is this mindset that empowers entrepreneurs to embrace change, overcome obstacles, and consistently rise to the challenges that mark the path to success.

Building on the pillars of adaptability, creativity, and resilience, the next step is fostering continuous learning and curiosity to thrive in an ever-changing business environment.

These traits not only fuel innovation but also empower entrepreneurs to transform challenges into opportunities for growth and advancement.

With a solid understanding of adaptability, creativity, and resilience as cornerstones of the entrepreneurial mindset, it's time to explore how these elements translate into real-world business practices.

As we move forward, we'll uncover how embracing experimentation alongside adaptability not only mitigates challenges but also unlocks exciting new avenues for growth in the ever-evolving business landscape.

Reflective Question:

How have you demonstrated adaptability in your career so far, and what lessons have you learned from these experiences?

EXPERIMENTATION AND ADAPTABILITY

In the fast-paced world of entrepreneurship, experimentation and adaptability transcend mere survival—they're essential for growth and innovation.

According to a study by DB Insights, which analyzed 101 startup post-mortems:

42% of startups failed due to a lack of market need for their product or service. This statistic highlights that many startups fail not because of poor execution, but because they fail to adapt to what the market actually needs.

Successful entrepreneurs must be willing and able to modify their initial visions based on market feedback.

They also need to adapt to changing market conditions and their audience's needs and desires.

Experimentation helps businesses find success.

By testing and refining ideas, businesses identify what truly resonates with their market.

Adaptability in navigating ever-shifting terrains ensures that businesses not only withstand changes but thrive in them.

THE POWER OF EXPERIMENTATION

Experimentation drives growth by allowing businesses to test hypotheses about their products, services, or operations in real-world settings.

This iterative approach ensures that strategies are not based on assumptions but on actual market responses and data.

Consider the story of Dropbox, which initially launched as a simple online storage solution for individuals.

Through rigorous user testing and beta releases, they discovered how crucial ease-of-use was, pivoting their focus towards seamless integration and usability.

This approach allowed them to scale rapidly, proving their model before investing heavily in infrastructure.

Experimentation also encourages innovation.

By fostering a culture that encourages safe experimentation, companies often uncover hidden niches or entirely new market opportunities previously unexplored.

ADAPTING IN A CHANGING MARKET

Adaptability is vital for sustaining growth in today's constantly evolving market landscape.

The COVID-19 pandemic underscored the critical need for businesses to pivot swiftly to survive.

Many restaurants, unable to serve customers in their dining rooms, pivoted to delivery and takeout models, with some even embarking on virtual kitchens to meet shifting food delivery trends.

A notable story of adaptability comes from a yoga studio in New York City.

When faced with closure due to lockdowns, the studio rapidly transitioned from in-person classes to a robust online streaming platform.

This pivot not only helped retain their loyal clientele but also attracted a global audience, turning a local business into an international online hub.

Similarly, a small restaurant famous for its breakfast menu capitalized on the pandemic's challenges by launching a "Brunch Box" delivery service.

They included not just meals, but also unique, homemade sauces and pastries that customers adored.

This pivot retained regulars and garnished new clientele, ultimately increasing their revenue streams and helping them thrive during a difficult period.

These stories illustrate the profound power of adaptability.

By adjusting business models in response to changing circumstances, these businesses not only survived current challenges but also laid a strong foundation for continued success and expansion.

These examples underscore how adaptability not only ensures survival during challenging times, but also creates opportunities for lasting innovation and growth.

LEARNING FROM SMALL BUSINESS ADAPTATION

Small businesses often serve as the most agile and innovative examples of adaptability.

One illustrative case is the story of a local bakery originally known for its artisan breads.

During a downturn, the bakery began experimenting with offering baking classes and selling sourdough starters alongside their loaves.

These changes not only captured a new segment of aspiring home bakers but also established a new revenue stream that sustained the business through challenging economic conditions.

Both experimentation and adaptability are key to growing a business into a sustainable venture.

They are interlinked disciplines that allow businesses to evolve continuously, ensuring they remain relevant and competitive.

By learning from real-world examples and embracing these philosophies, entrepreneurs can craft resilient strategies that drive long-term success.

As you harness the power of experimentation and adaptability, the next critical piece in the entrepreneurial puzzle is learning resilience through failure.

While the spirit of innovation sets a promising stage, success also relies heavily on the capacity to face and learn from setbacks.

Resilience not only safeguards your business's stability, but also acts as a driving force for growth and renewed purpose.

ACTION EXERCISE:

Identify one area where you can pivot in your business.

List three strategies you could use (or have used) to address unexpected challenges.

Resilience Through Failure

In entrepreneurship, resilience turns setbacks into opportunities for growth and innovation.

Steve's journey from engineer to tech consultant demonstrates how resilience can transform challenges into opportunities. Despite early difficulties in marketing his services, he persevered.

Instead, Steve leveraged client feedback to refine his approach, align his services with specific market needs, and gradually build a loyal customer base.

His story illustrates that resilience involves using each setback (or "failure") as a springboard for innovation and improvement.

Resilience is a trait shared by many successful entrepreneurs, from small business owners to industry pioneers.

Real-Life Case Study: Thomas Edison

Consider Thomas Edison, whose relentless pursuit of the electric light bulb was met with many unsuccessful attempts before achieving success.

He famously stated, "I have not failed. I've just found 10,000 ways that won't work."

Edison's mindset demonstrates how resilience and perseverance can turn repeated failures into groundbreaking successes.

Strategies to Foster Resilience

- Reflect and Learn:

- After each setback, take time to reflect and analyze what went wrong and why.

- Stay Persistent:

- Keep sight of your long-term goals. Each failure is a step in the journey.

- Seek Support:

- Connect with mentors and peers to gain fresh perspectives and encouragement.

Embracing resilience helps you navigate the unpredictable world of entrepreneurship, finding stability amid chaos and using every fall as a learning experience to rise stronger and more determined.

Cultivating resilience lays a foundation for continuous learning, creativity, and curiosity—key drivers of sustained momentum and success in ever-changing markets.

Building resilience through failure provides a solid foundation for growth; it's the springboard that propels you into a phase of deeper learning and innovation.

As you navigate challenges with newfound strength, embracing continuous learning, creativity, and curiosity becomes essential to sustaining momentum and staying ahead in evolving markets.

Let's see how they fit into the entrepreneurial mindset.

Reflective Question:

When faced with a setback, do you see it as a chance to learn and explore new possibilities?

CONTINUOUS LEARNING, CREATIVITY, AND CURIOSITY

In today's rapidly changing entrepreneurial landscape, continuous learning and curiosity are essential tools for success.

They not only drive personal growth but also propel businesses to innovate and thrive in competitive markets.

Creativity is equally vital, serving as the engine of innovation and driving new ideas forward.

Creativity can transform knowledge and curiosity into practical and novel business solutions that ensure growth and sustainability.

Lifelong Learning: The Entrepreneur's Edge

Early in his career, Steve recognized that lifelong learning was essential for transitioning from engineering to tech consulting.

By using resources like Coursera and Udemy, he kept his skills updated, enabling him to offer cutting-edge solutions to his clients.

These tools helped him explore new fields such as digital strategy—how businesses use online resources and technologies to reach their goals—and project management, which involves planning and overseeing projects to ensure they are completed efficiently and effectively.

This significantly expanded his service offerings, enabling him to deliver greater value to his clients.

Creativity: The Catalyst for Growth

Creativity extends beyond art and aesthetics; in business, it is the driving force behind advancement and problem-solving.

In business, it's about finding new ways to solve problems and meet customer needs.

It allows entrepreneurs to see beyond conventional limits and use insights from various fields to forge original approaches.

For Steve, creativity involved developing innovative solutions tailored to his clients' unique challenges, setting his services apart in a competitive market.

Real-World Example: Creativity in Healthcare

The Cleveland Clinic's Heart and Vascular Institute offers a compelling example of how creativity drives innovation in healthcare.

Facing the challenge of integrating cutting-edge technologies to enhance patient care, the institute developed new protocols using mobile health technologies.

By implementing these protocols, the clinic enabled remote monitoring for patients with chronic heart conditions, leading to improved outcomes and higher satisfaction rates.

By creatively employing technology, the clinic streamlined their patient monitoring processes and reduced hospital readmissions.

This change in strategy showed how creative problem-solving can lead to substantial improvements in service delivery and patient care.

This innovation highlights the transformative power of creativity in healthcare, enabling institutions to tackle critical challenges and maintain leadership in medical care.

Real-Life Learning Success Story

Another inspiring example is Eric Yuan, the founder of Zoom.

Initially, Eric faced numerous obstacles in establishing his video conferencing platform.

However, his commitment to constantly learning and adapting to new technologies and user feedback led to Zoom becoming a household name, especially during the global shift to remote work in 2020.

Inspired by Yuna's dedication, Steve recognized the importance of continuously upgrading his skills in emerging technologies.

The Role of Curiosity in Innovation

Curiosity sparks the drive to explore new possibilities and ask critical questions, often leading to groundbreaking innovations.

Just as Steve's inquisitiveness about the tech world led him to start his consultancy, it was the same sense of curiosity that transformed Airbnb's founders' idea of shared living spaces into a groundbreaking business model in the hospitality industry.

Practical Strategies for Learning and Growth

- Set Learning Goals:

- Pinpoint areas for growth and establish clear, actionable learning objectives.

- For instance, Steve aimed to enhance his digital marketing skills by committing to specific courses, a strategy that could be applied universally.

- Embrace Failures:

- Both Steve and many other successful entrepreneurs view failures as learning opportunities.

- Each setback offers valuable lessons that refine strategies and improve decision-making.

As we cultivate continuous learning, creativity, and curiosity, these elements not only fuel innovation but also lay the groundwork for building confidence—a crucial component in the entrepreneurial journey.

This confidence enables you to lead with conviction, inspire your team, and make informed decisions that shape your business landscape.

ACTION EXERCISE:

How can you integrate continuous learning into your current professional routine?

Think about a current challenge your business faces. What creative solutions can you think of that go beyond the traditional approaches?

Identify a new field or technology that you're curious about. How can exploring this technology drive innovation and growth in your business?

Confidence and Leadership

Confidence is the foundation of effective decision-making and leadership in entrepreneurship.

It drives entrepreneurs to make bold decisions and remain steadfast amid uncertainty.

This confidence not only affects how you operate but also deeply influences your team, customers, and potential collaborators.

THE ROLE OF CONFIDENCE IN DECISION-MAKING

Confidence in decision-making empowers entrepreneurs to act decisively and pursue opportunities with conviction.

When you're confident, you trust in your own abilities and vision, making it easier to take calculated risks and push boundaries.

This doesn't mean ignoring potential obstacles but rather having the courage to address them head-on, knowing that each decision is a vital step toward your ultimate goals.

Confidence is not only an internal asset, but also a tool that shapes how others perceive and respond to your leadership.

INSPIRING TEAMS AND CUSTOMERS

A confident leader motivates their team by fostering an environment where creativity and innovation flourish.

When you exude self-assurance, it instills faith in your leadership, encouraging team members to contribute ideas and take ownership of their work.

Such an environment fosters collaboration and propels the entire team toward collective success.

Confidence resonates not only with your team but also with customers and potential collaborators.

People are naturally drawn to businesses led by individuals who believe in their mission and future.

This can help convert potential clients into loyal customers and make collaborators eager to join forces with you.

They see your vision and are compelled to be a part of it, knowing they're partnering with someone who is committed and capable

CULTIVATING CONFIDENCE AS A LEADER

Embrace Learning:

- Continuously expand your knowledge and skills.
- The more informed you are, the more confident you'll feel.

Acknowledge Success:

- Celebrate your achievements, however small.

- Recognizing progress boosts morale and reinforces your capacity to lead effectively.

Seek Feedback:

- Encourage open communication and constructive feedback from your team.

- This not only helps you grow but demonstrates your commitment to ongoing improvement.

Practice Self-Reflection:

- Dedicate time to evaluate your leadership decisions and personal growth.

- Understanding your strengths and areas for improvement builds a deeper sense of self-assurance.

Confidence and leadership are pivotal elements of the entrepreneurial mindset.

They enable you to steer your business with clarity and inspire those around you to pursue innovation and excellence.

With confidence and leadership setting the stage for an inspiring journey, the next step is to actively cultivate these qualities into your daily practice.

Implementing practical strategies helps you nurture adaptability, creativity, and resilience as you work toward your goals.

Let's explore some practical steps you can take to build this mindset into your daily practice, ensuring it becomes a natural part of your entrepreneurial journey.

ACTION EXERCISE:

Reflect on your entrepreneurial strengths and list them.

Identify three areas for growth that you'd like to focus on in the coming year.

PRACTICAL STEPS TO BUILD THE MINDSET

Developing an entrepreneurial mindset demands intentional action and consistent practice.

Here are some practical steps you can take to integrate adaptability, creativity, and resilience into your daily life.

GOAL SETTING

Defining clear, achievable goals is essential to steering an entrepreneurial journey.

It creates a roadmap, helping you focus on what truly matters while measuring your progress along the way.

Start with your big vision and break it down into smaller, achievable milestones.

This not only makes large goals seem more manageable but also provides opportunities to celebrate incremental achievements, boosting motivation and confidence.

EXAMPLE IN PRACTICE: SARA BLAKELY

The story of Sara Blakely, founder of Spanx, exemplifies how goal setting can drive entrepreneurial success.

Her journey began with the simple goal of creating comfortable and seamless undergarments.

Despite having no background in fashion design, Sara was determined to revolutionize the industry.

She set specific, strategic goals to guide her path from idea to execution.

Starting with the design and prototype phase, she then moved on to patenting her product, securing production, and developing a marketing strategy.

Her goals were not just end results; they were carefully mapped steps that allowed her to penetrate a traditionally male-dominated industry.

Through her focused approach, Sara not only overcame numerous challenges but also successfully positioned Spanx as a leading global brand in intimate apparel.

CELEBRATING SMALL WINS

Celebrating small victories is a powerful strategy to sustain momentum and uplift morale.

Whether it's launching a new product or overcoming a minor hurdle, acknowledging progress reinforces the hard work and commitment of you and your team.

EXAMPLE IN PRACTICE: RICHARD BRANSON

Richard Branson, the founder of the Virgin Group, consistently emphasizes the importance of celebrating achievements, no matter how small, to foster innovation and ambition within his teams.

Branson believes that taking time to acknowledge accomplishments boosts morale and creates a positive corporate culture.

At Virgin, celebrations are integral to their business model, encouraging creativity and motivation.

By recognizing even modest successes, Branson ensures his teams maintain enthusiasm, drive, and a continuous forward momentum, all crucial elements in an environment geared toward groundbreaking ideas and risk-taking.

EMBRACING COMMUNITY CONNECTIONS

Building a network of supportive relationships is essential for growth and resilience.

Engaging with other entrepreneurs, mentors, and industry professionals provides a wealth of insights and encouragement.

Surround yourself with people who inspire you and challenge you to grow.

EXAMPLE IN PRACTICE: TIM FERRISS

Tim Ferriss, renowned entrepreneur and author of "The 4-Hour Workweek," attributes much of his success to his proactive cultivation of a diverse and influential community.

Ferriss actively seeks connections with mentors and peers who offer new perspectives and opportunities.

Through his relationships, he tapped into a reservoir of collective wisdom, which he used to fuel his ventures.

By listening to a myriad of voices, Tim ensures he's continuously challenging his assumptions, exploring new methodologies, and expanding his business horizons.

By incorporating these practical steps of goal setting, celebrating small wins, embracing community connections, as illustrated by these inspiring narratives, you lay the groundwork for a robust entrepreneurial mindset.

By integrating these strategies into your daily practices, you can navigate challenges with resilience, seize opportunities with creativity, and create lasting success.

As we conclude this chapter, let's revisit how these components fit into the broader journey of personal growth and professional success through cultivating an Entrepreneurial Mindset.

ACTION EXERCISE:

What long-term goal do you envision for your business growth?

Reflect on a recent success, big or small. How did you celebrate, and how did it affect your morale and motivation?

Identify someone in your network—or someone you'd like to connect with—who could offer valuable insights or support.

Conclusion: A Journey of Growth

As we conclude this chapter, let's reflect on the journey of developing a resilient entrepreneurial mindset—an essential tool for professionals embarking on new ventures.

Thriving in entrepreneurship—especially for those over 50—requires embracing adaptability, creativity, and resilience as core pillars of success.

These qualities help you navigate challenges, embrace opportunities, and sustain growth in an ever-changing business landscape.

Throughout this chapter, we've explored practical strategies to develop this mindset, such as setting clear goals, celebrating small wins, and building connections with a community of support.

By adopting these strategies—illustrated through the inspiring journeys of Sara Blakely, Richard Branson, and Tim Ferriss—you lay a solid foundation for lasting success in both your personal and professional life.

Steve's story reminds us that lifelong learning and adaptability can turn a personal passion—such as his love for technology—into a thriving consultancy business.

His journey shows how resilience turns challenges into stepping stones for greater achievements.

Moreover, cultivating an entrepreneurial mindset extends far beyond personal success. It enables you to create solutions that address pressing societal challenges, improve the quality of life for others, and inspire a ripple effect of creativity and innovation in your industry.

As entrepreneurs, the innovations and solutions you develop can address pressing real-world issues, improve lives, and inspire a broader wave of creativity and problem-solving.

Remember, this mindset isn't just about business—it's about building an approach to life that welcomes growth in every dimension.

As you forge ahead on this path, remain committed to adaptability, nurture creative thinking, and strengthen resilience.

Together, these elements will empower you to drive meaningful change—not just within your business, but also across your community and industry.

By fostering innovation and collaboration, you can inspire your peers and set a powerful example for future generations of entrepreneurs.

With a resilient entrepreneurial mindset in place, the next step is exploring how your journey can create meaningful impact, both personally and within your broader community.

In Chapter 11, we will explore how entrepreneurship provides not only financial rewards but also personal satisfaction and societal contributions, paving the way for creating a purposeful business.

CHAPTER 11

IMPACT AND FULFILLMENT THROUGH ENTREPRENEURSHIP

In today's fast-changing economy, a powerful trend has emerged: over half of new businesses in the United States are founded by professionals aged 50 and older.

And a significant number of them are 55 and older.

Many of these entrepreneurs, including a significant number aged 50 and older, find that starting a business offers a fulfilling way to share their passions and expertise while creating a lasting impact and pursuing personal satisfaction in a new phase of life.

Let's explore how aligning your business with personal values can create profound fulfillment and drive meaningful impact.

INTRODUCTION: ALIGNING PURPOSE WITH PROFIT

Meet Bernie, a visionary who redefined success by blending his financial acumen with a deep passion for social good.

His story demonstrates how professionals at any stage of life can align their skills with a meaningful mission.

After years of climbing the corporate ladder in finance, Bernie reached a crossroads.

Despite his accolades and financial success, he yearned for deeper meaning in his work

Mentoring at local shelters showed Bernie the profound fulfillment of making a difference in others' lives.

This realization ignited a transformation.

Bernie decided to channel his expertise into establishing a community lending platform.

This journey offers a practical roadmap for professionals over 50 considering side hustle businesses.

It demonstrates how one can effectively merge personal values with professional skills to pursue rewarding ventures.

More than a conventional business venture, Bernie's platform aimed to empower underserved communities by providing access to opportunities that were once out of reach, such as affordable loans and financial education.

Bernie's venture was driven by purpose rather than profit—a mission to align progress with heartfelt passion.

Bernie's story is more than an individual journey; it's a testament to the powerful impact entrepreneurship can have when intertwined with social objectives.

Entrepreneurs like Bernie exemplify how businesses can transcend traditional financial metrics to become catalysts for transformative societal change.

Through his efforts, Bernie not only redefined his own success but also contributed to a broader narrative: that personal fulfillment and societal impact are the ultimate rewards of a purpose-driven entrepreneurial path.

Bernie's journey underscores the broader benefits of building a purpose-driven business—one that not only achieves financial success, but also creates lasting social impact.

From enhancing personal satisfaction to effecting substantial societal transformation, entrepreneurship rooted in passion offers a roadmap to creating a legacy that resonates far beyond the bottom line.

As we learn from Bernie's inspiring journey, the integration of passion and purpose into business endeavors sets the stage for remarkable societal transformations.

In this next section, we'll delve into the concept of social entrepreneurship, exploring how it blends innovation and purpose to address pressing societal challenges while fostering both personal fulfillment and community wellbeing.

WHAT IS SOCIAL ENTREPRENEURSHIP?

Social entrepreneurship involves innovatively addressing societal challenges through business ventures that balance meaningful impact with financial sustainability.

Unlike traditional business models focused solely on financial gain, social entrepreneurship combines business strategies with a mission to tackle challenges such as inequality, environmental issues, and community upliftment.

A compelling example of this approach is found in the story of TOMS Shoes, a company that redefined the balance between profit and purpose.

TOMS Shoes is a perfect illustration of this concept.

Blake Mycoskie is the founder of TOMS Shoes.

During a visit to Argentina, Mycoskie saw many children without shoes and recognized a critical need that he could address.

This sparked the creation of TOMS Shoes with its pioneering "One for One" model, donating a pair of shoes for every pair sold.

This social entrepreneurship model has provided millions of shoes to those in need, proving that businesses can successfully balance profit with purpose.

Blake's story emphasizes the essence of social entrepreneurship: it's not just about financial rewards but also the fulfillment and societal impact that come from building businesses with a conscientious mission.

Through these examples, we see how embedding social objectives within business models enhances personal satisfaction while fostering broader societal transformations.

As Blake demonstrated, social entrepreneurship is not only about creating innovative solutions but also about laying the groundwork for real, positive changes within communities.

This natural progression from addressing societal challenges to enhancing communal value underscores the true potential of purpose-driven business models.

Let's delve deeper into how these ventures enrich the business world while creating tangible, lasting value for the communities they serve.

This reinforces the idea that true fulfillment goes hand-in-hand with fostering positive change.

CREATING COMMUNITY VALUE

Social enterprises stand apart by creating tangible benefits for their communities, focusing on value creation rather than solely maximizing profits.

These businesses play a pivotal role in addressing local challenges while fostering economic resilience.

Unlike traditional businesses, these enterprises reinvest their earnings into local communities, driving growth and resilience.

Take Bernie's initiative, for example.

He provided critical financial services to underserved areas while reinvesting earnings into local development projects. These efforts fostered economic growth and empowered individuals within the community.

This reinvestment model acts as a catalyst for sustainable community development, demonstrating the profound impact that businesses can have when they focus on broader social goals.

Consider another remarkable story, that of Warby Parker, a company committed to offering affordable eyewear.

For every pair of glasses sold, the company donates another pair to individuals in need through nonprofit partners, enhancing vision and creating new opportunities for education and economic growth.

This initiative does more than enhance vision; it improves educational outcomes and economic possibilities for recipients, creating a ripple effect of positive change.

Social enterprises often support education programs, offering scholarships or investing in local schools.

These initiatives empower young minds, equipping students with skills essential for future success.

Sustainable practices, such as adopting eco-friendly manufacturing processes, not only benefit the environment but also encourage a culture of responsibility and stewardship within communities.

This holistic approach to business underscores a powerful truth: by weaving community-focused strategies into their operations, social entrepreneurs can transform local landscapes, cultivating a thriving ecosystem that supports people, the planet, and prosperity.

By evolving to meet societal needs, businesses are redefining success, championing a future where economic growth aligns seamlessly with social progress for the greater good.

Joan Steltmann: Bounce Children's Foundation

Joan Steltmann provides a compelling example.

Her story exemplifies the profound impact of purpose-driven entrepreneurship at age 50.

At 50, with two decades of experience as a tech industry marketing executive, Joan began a transformative journey by founding Bounce Children's Foundation.

Bounce Children's Foundation is a non-profit organization dedicated to supporting chronically ill children and their families. The foundation empowers children to build resilience and thrive, emphasizing a focus on thriving rather than merely surviving.

Joan's shift to the nonprofit sector reflected her heartfelt mission to channel professional expertise into meaningful societal impact.

With a commitment to enriching community well-being, businesses harness the true power of entrepreneurship by transforming lives and landscapes.

Next, we explore how impact-driven enterprises integrate social and financial goals, demonstrating how innovative business models drive societal advancement and personal fulfillment.

IMPACT-ORIENTED BUSINESS MODELS

In today's transformative economy, impact-oriented business models are redefining success by seamlessly weaving together social objectives and economic ambitions.

These businesses demonstrate that financial performance and social impact can coexist and even enhance one another.

Greyston Bakery:

A pioneer in this realm, Greyston Bakery embodies the essence of combining purpose with profit.

By adopting an open hiring policy, they offer jobs to anyone willing to work, regardless of their background.

This approach has fueled the company's revenue growth while providing opportunities for hundreds who were previously marginalized.

Through their efforts, Greyston has documented significant reductions in local unemployment rates and improved community well-being, illustrating the profound impact such business models can have.

Bernie's Community Lending:

Guided by a vision of equal opportunity, Bernie's venture combines financial expertise with social responsibility.

By offering affordable loans to those typically excluded from conventional banking, his platform not only generates revenue but also fosters community empowerment and economic resilience.

The measure of success for Bernie is not solely in profits but in the tangible improvements in his clients' lives, such as increased financial literacy and home ownership rates.

TOMS Shoes:

Another excellent example is TOMS, which has married social impact with its business model through the "One for One" initiative.

For every product sold, a product is donated to someone in need.

This approach has led to the donation of millions of shoes and eyewear, improving health and educational outcomes across the globe.

The direct correlation between sales and social benefit exemplifies how businesses can achieve growth while creating substantial societal value.

These examples show that impact-oriented business models provide a blueprint for companies aspiring to achieve more than just financial success.

Embedding social goals into core strategies fosters inclusivity and sustainability, paving the way for a more equitable and prosperous world.

This alignment of impact with profit not only satisfies shareholders but also nurtures an era of entrepreneurship that prioritizes both individual and collective benefit.

As we've seen, aligning business operations with broader societal goals can profoundly transform communities while driving economic success.

As an example of their impact on society, some of the large companies have been inspired by the societal impact and growth potential for their own companies based on TOMS' "One for One" initiative.

In 2010-2011, SKECHERS created a canvas shoe similar to TOMS' shoes. They called it BOBS ("Benefitting Others By Shoes").

SKECHERS planned to donate two pairs of shoes for each pair of BOBS sold.

Since 2012, TOMS has donated over 16 million pairs of shoes, supporting children affected by natural disasters and poverty in more than 60 countries worldwide.

Having explored the power of impact-oriented business models, let's turn to how personal aspirations can intersect with purposeful business strategies to drive meaningful change.

Aligning your passions with your work not only enhances personal fulfillment but also magnifies your influence, driving meaningful societal change and showcasing entrepreneurship's true power.

ALIGNING PASSIONS WITH PURPOSE

Entrepreneurs flourish when they align their personal passions with their business goals, creating ventures that generate profit while driving meaningful societal change.

This alignment creates a deep sense of fulfillment, as entrepreneurs find meaning in their work by contributing positively to the world.

Bernie, as previously discussed, combined his financial expertise in finance with a passion for social justice.

By focusing on financial empowerment for underserved communities, Bernie not only fulfilled a personal calling but also brought about considerable social value.

A remarkable case is that of Yvon Chouinard, founder of Patagonia.

Motivated by a deep love for the environment, Yvon Chouinard founded Patagonia, embedding sustainability into the company's core operations.

Patagonia also commits 1% of its sales to environmental causes through its "1% for the Planet" initiative, further demonstrating how personal ethics can align with corporate strategies to effect global change.

Patagonia's commitment to reducing its ecological footprint reflects how aligning business operations with personal ethics can lead to unprecedented brand loyalty and environmental impact.

Jessica Jackley, co-founder of Kiva, provides another inspiring example.

Her passion for global development inspired her to create Kiva, a platform facilitating microloans to entrepreneurs in developing regions.

By connecting lenders with entrepreneurs, Kiva has transformed countless lives, while allowing Jessica to live her values through her business endeavors.

As of 2023, the Kiva community has facilitated over 5 million loans, totalling more than $176 million.

Then there's Nonna Nerina, a remarkable example of a retiree who successfully started an online business in her golden years.

An Italian grandmother, Nonna became the beloved face of "Nonna Live," an online cooking class business that she created during the challenges of the COVID-19 pandemic.

She combined her cherished family recipes and extensive culinary knowledge to create a virtual platform that resonated with students worldwide.

Though she has passed away, Nonna legacy lives on through her business, which now employs other retired Italian grandmothers to teach authentic recipes.

Through these examples, we see that when entrepreneurs align their ventures with their passions, they unlock the potential to achieve both personal satisfaction and societal progress.

This fusion of personal ambition and social responsibility not only enriches the entrepreneur's journey but also contributes to crafting a world that benefits from sustainable and compassionate business practices.

As entrepreneurs align their passions with business pursuits, they set the stage for more holistic success.

The next step focuses on balancing the triple bottom line—people, planet, and profit—ensuring that their ventures contribute positively to every aspect of society while achieving sustainable growth.

Let's explore how this balanced approach fosters deep-rooted success and societal wellbeing.

BALANCING THE TRIPLE BOTTOM LINE

Achieving success in today's world requires more than just financial gains.

Nowadays, success entails a holistic approach that balances people, planet, and profit.

This "Triple Bottom Line" framework ensures that businesses thrive while contributing positively to society and the environment.

This holistic framework challenges businesses to evaluate success through a lens that prioritizes long-term societal and environmental wellbeing alongside financial performance.

People:

At the heart of this framework is the commitment to social equity and community impact.

Companies like TOMS have shown how business success can directly translate into social benefits.

Their "One for One" model not only boosts sales but also provides tangible benefits like footwear and eyewear to those in need, illustrating a direct connection between business activity and social impact.

Planet:

Environmental stewardship plays a central role in the triple bottom line, emphasizing sustainable practices that benefit both businesses and the planet.

Patagonia exemplifies sustainable business practices by prioritizing eco-friendly production processes and encouraging customers to consider the environmental impact of their consumption.

Through initiatives like responsible sourcing and effective recycling programs, the company demonstrates how operations can seamlessly align with environmental values.

Profit:

Economic sustainability is an essential pillar of the triple bottom line. By balancing financial health with ethical responsibility, businesses can leverage profits to advance social and environmental causes.

By integrating these values into their economic models, companies like Patagonia and TOMS demonstrate that it is indeed viable to achieve profitability while maintaining high ethical standards.

These examples illustrate the powerful impact a balanced approach can have.

By prioritizing the triple bottom line, businesses not only strengthen their public image, but also build enduring legacies that enrich communities and protect the planet for future generations.

This model underscores the potential of entrepreneurship to lead the way in creating a sustainable and equitable future.

By adopting a balanced approach that values people, the planet, and profit, businesses lay the foundation for enduring success.

Let's now explore how entrepreneurs can amplify their impact by building legacies that transcend financial metrics, with a focus on mentorship, ethical leadership, and community empowerment.

ACTION EXERCISE:

1. Assess your current business strategy to identify opportunities for balancing people, planet, and profit.

2. Define clear, actionable goals with specific objectives for each component of the triple bottom line.

BUILDING A LEGACY BEYOND FINANCIAL SUCCESS

Creating a lasting entrepreneurial impact goes beyond financial success, focusing on mentorship, knowledge sharing, and ethical leadership to drive business growth and societal advancement.

Mentorship:

Entrepreneurs like Richard Branson of Virgin have shown the power of mentorship in shaping the next generation of leaders.

Branson's commitment to mentoring his team has driven innovation within Virgin while inspiring leaders worldwide to embrace creativity and ethics.

His mentorship extends beyond his organization, exemplified by his involvement in initiatives like the Branson Centre for Entrepreneurship, which nurtures emerging business leaders.

By investing time in guiding others, entrepreneurs can perpetuate a culture of collaboration and continuous learning, ensuring their values and vision endure long-term.

Knowledge Sharing:

Ray Dalio, founder of Bridgewater Associates, exemplifies the impact of knowledge sharing.

Bridgewater Associates is a global investment management firm that advises institutional clients and private investment funds. Founded in 1975 by Ray Dalio, Bridgewater is known for pioneering risk budgeting..

Ray Dalio fosters radical transparency at Bridgewater Associates, encouraging open dialogue and a culture of learning from mistakes, which strengthens the company's foundation.

His approach is outlined in his book Principles, offering actionable insights for entrepreneurs seeking to implement similar strategies.

This approach allows for a mutual exchange of ideas, driving both personal and organizational growth. Entrepreneurs who prioritize sharing expertise create ecosystems where everyone learns and benefits, further extending their influence and legacy.

Ethical Leadership:

Anita Roddick, founder of The Body Shop, used ethical leadership to build a business committed to societal values.

The Body Shop exemplifies ethical leadership, striving for a world that is not only more beautiful, but also more equitable and fair.

Under Anita Roddick's visionary leadership, the company champions social activism and ethical practices.

Every product and business decision reflects a steadfast dedication to empowering women and girls, fostering equality, and creating opportunities through the Community Fair Trade program.

This is more than a business model—it represents a movement dedicated to driving meaningful change.

Her trailblazing efforts in sustainability and social responsibility established new industry standards and catalyzed global shifts in consumer behavior.

Roddick's unwavering commitment to ethical business practices ensured her company's positive societal contributions, creating an enduring impact that transcended profit margins.

By embracing mentorship, knowledge sharing, and ethical leadership, entrepreneurs can build legacies that profoundly influence their industries and communities.

These principles not only enhance business success, but also foster lasting connections and promote a culture of ethical entrepreneurship capable of transforming societies.

Cultivating such a legacy ensures that the essence of entrepreneurship—driving meaningful change—extends far beyond financial metrics.

Having explored how entrepreneurs can create enduring legacies through mentorship and ethical leadership, it's essential to consider the broader role they play as global citizens.

Let's examine how embracing global responsibility can amplify a business's impact, contributing not only to local communities but also to societal progress on an international scale.

GLOBAL CITIZENSHIP AND RESPONSIBILITY

In today's interconnected world, even small businesses possess the potential to drive significant global change.

Entrepreneurs today have unparalleled opportunities to create meaningful global impact.

Embracing the role of global citizens requires considering how business actions influence not only local communities, but also the broader global landscape.

The Entrepreneur's Global Role:

Operating a home-based digital marketing business as a professional over 50 enables you to share your passions and expertise on a global scale.

By leveraging your knowledge and expertise, you can educate and inspire a worldwide audience, creating content that resonates far beyond your local area.

Through digital platforms, you have the power to connect with people everywhere, exchanging ideas and fostering a rich community of learning and growth.

Your business can serve as a model for sustainable practices and lifelong learning, illustrating how small ventures can make a lasting global impact by disseminating valuable insights and building meaningful connections.

The Power of Collaborations:

Collaborating is essential for driving meaningful change on a global scale.

By partnering with global organizations and nonprofits, small businesses can pool resources and expertise to address pressing challenges such as poverty and renewable energy.

These partnerships allow for shared knowledge and resources, helping businesses grow their impact and create sustainable change.

Compelling Case Studies:

Kay Miller's transition into digital marketing at age 50 highlights the transformative power of leveraging global platforms such as LinkedIn.

With its current vast reach spanning over 200 countries and territories, LinkedIn has come a long way since 2002, when it was created, and in 2003, when it was launched online.

At that time LinkedIn started as a small professional networking platform.

It started as a professional social networking site, allowing people to connect with other people in their industry and share job opportunities.

Drawing from her extensive corporate experience, Kay focused on mastering LinkedIn's unique features and capabilities.

Offering a platform that would resonate with people across the globe, LinkedIn has grown to one of the most distinguished networking sites for professionals worldwide.

Kay's story is a testament to the power of experience and specialization.

By concentrating on LinkedIn, she tapped into a world-wide network, demonstrating that age is an asset when combined with expertise, passion, and the right digital tools.

Her adaptability and commitment to lifelong learning have kept her at the forefront of digital marketing trends.

For professionals over 50, Kay's journey serves as an inspiring reminder that it's never too late to transform expertise into a thriving, globally impactful venture.

Fair Trade Impact:

The Fair Trade movement exemplifies how equity and sustainability in business practices can lead to significant global advancements.

By embracing these principles, entrepreneurs contribute to global development, fostering an environment where businesses uplift communities while thriving economically.

By practicing responsible stewardship and fostering strategic collaborations, entrepreneurs drive both business success and meaningful contributions to societal progress.

By embracing their role on the global stage, they help shape a more equitable and sustainable future, ensuring their legacy of impact extends across continents and generations.

The Solo, Home-Based Entrepreneur:

Home-based entrepreneurs have the power to create meaningful global impact by leveraging digital platforms and international networks.

Digital platforms and global networks enable home-based entrepreneurs to participate in international commerce, offering distinctive products or services that reach beyond local boundaries.

These entrepreneurs have the opportunity to incorporate sustainable practices into their business models and participate in global causes through collaborations and online communities.

By thoughtfully choosing suppliers, advocating for fair trade, and using eco-friendly packaging, even small businesses can champion responsible entrepreneurship.

By embracing their roles as global citizens, solo entrepreneurs help foster an interconnected business ecosystem where every decision creates a ripple of positive global impact.

They exemplify how impactful entrepreneurship is accessible to all, regardless of scale, fostering a legacy of purpose and shared prosperity that transcends borders.

Through responsible stewardship and strategic collaboration, entrepreneurs not only drive business success but also contribute to the greater good.

By embracing their role on the global stage, they help shape a more equitable and sustainable future, ensuring their legacy of impact extends across continents and generations.

As we've journeyed through the diverse facets of entrepreneurship, we've seen how impactful actions can create a legacy of positive change.

Now, let's conclude by revisiting how these substantial impacts provide not only financial rewards but also profound personal fulfillment, cementing the true essence of purpose-driven entrepreneurship.

CONCLUSION: IMPACT AS FULFILLMENT

Reflecting on the multifaceted nature of entrepreneurship reveals that its true rewards go well beyond financial success.

Bernie's journey highlighted how aligning personal passions with purposeful missions not only enables businesses to thrive economically, but also contributes significantly to societal good.

This dual focus provides entrepreneurs with deep satisfaction and a profound sense of fulfillment that transcends traditional success.

Key actionable insights remind us that success involves:

Social Entrepreneurship:

- Innovating with intention to meet societal needs while achieving financial stability.

Creating Community Value:

- Reinvesting in localities to drive both economic growth and community empowerment.

Balancing the Triple Bottom Line:

- Achieving a harmonious balance among profits, people, and the planet ensures long-term sustainability.

Building a Legacy:

- Going beyond immediate gains by engaging in mentorship, knowledge sharing, and ethical leadership.

Embracing Global Citizenship:

Recognizing today's interconnected world and fostering international collaborations to foster broader global impact.

Bernie's transformation offers a roadmap for professionals over 50 who are seeking to infuse fresh meaning and purpose into their careers.

Bernie's story inspires readers to identify their passions and harness their skills to drive change.

By adopting empathetic business strategies, they can achieve both personal fulfillment and a positive impact on their communities.

By daring to weave his financial expertise with his passion for social justice, Bernie crafted a legacy underscored by the power of community-focused endeavors.

For aspiring entrepreneurs, the challenge lies in envisioning the impact you wish to make and moving boldly towards it, confident that your entrepreneurial journey can offer extraordinary fulfillment and societal contribution.

This journey extends beyond career growth; it's about building a legacy uplifts and inspires.

As you embrace this path, bear in mind that mentorship and networking are pivotal.

They open doors to transformative opportunities.

Building strategic relationships, amplifies your social and business impact, driving your ventures to new heights.

Just as Bernie did, you have the potential to define success on your own terms, leaving a lasting imprint on the world.

ACTION EXERCISE:

1. Reflect on Your Interests and Skills: Consider what truly excites you and where your strengths lie.

2. List three skills or interests that you could turn into a business.

3. Define Your Core Values: Identify the values that are most important to you.

4. Reflect on the potential for your business ideas to have meaningful societal impact.

5. Craft a Vision Statement: Outline your business idea, emphasizing how it aligns your passion with broader societal needs. Let this vision serve as your guiding star in decision-making and growth.

Drawing from Bernie's journey, Chapter 12 underscores the vital role that mentorship and networking play in amplifying your business ventures and driving societal impact.

These strategic relationships are key to unlocking new opportunities and ensuring your entrepreneurial efforts continue to grow and make a difference.

CHAPTER 12

THE POWER OF MENTORSHIP AND NETWORKING

New Paths Unlocked: The Transformative of Power of Mentorship and Networking

Picture yourself at a crossroads, unsure of which direction to take—this was the exact scenario Bill Gates faced when weighing the prospect of mentorship from Warren Buffett.

Initially, Gates hesitated to pursue mentorship with Buffet, skeptical about how their vastly different industries—technology and investment—could connect.

Yet, he quickly discovered shared values in ethical business practices and philanthropy, forming the foundation for a transformative relationship.

By embracing the mentorship from Buffet, their relationship transformed skepticism into rich opportunities.

Their mentorship led to the creation of the "Giving Pledge," a campaign inspiring the wealthy to donate their fortunes to vital causes like education, healthcare, and poverty alleviation.

Bill Gates and Warren Buffett's story illustrates how mentorship doesn't just foster individual growth but can inspire transformative philanthropy.

What about professionals like Karen, a mid-level manager, or Bob, a finance expert?

How do professionals over 50 successfully pivot into new careers or ventures?

The secret often lies in the powerful dynamics of mentorship and networking.

Mentorship provides guidance through the wisdom of those who have walked the path before, while networking opens doors to new opportunities and meaningful connections.

Together, these forces can act as a launchpad for career transformation.

Let's talk about Karen and Bob. They offer inspiring stories of professionals who revitalized their careers by engaging with mentors and networks aligned with their new goals.

Take Karen, for instance—a mid-level manager who, at 52, redefined her career by transitioning into consulting.

Through targeted efforts like attending industry conferences and participating in professional online groups, Karen connected with mentors who provided invaluable advice and introduced her to potential clients.

These strategic relationships were pivotal in launching her thriving consultation career.

Similarly, Bob's story reveals how mentorship can help professionals chart entirely new paths in unfamiliar industries

Bob pivoted from a career in finance to the sustainable energy industry.

With the guidance of a mentor passionate about renewables, he gained critical industry knowledge, enabling a smooth and successful career shift.

For professionals over 50, embracing mentorship and strategic networking can unlock transformative career opportunities and unparalleled personal growth.

When researching Mentorship statistics for Professionals, I found that:

A 2017 survey by Moving Ahead revealed that 87% of mentees feel empowered through their mentoring relationships.

Studies suggest that 70% of individuals with mentors enjoy greater career success—a testament to the impactful nature of these relationships.

In this chapter, as we explore the realm of mentorship and networking further, we'll uncover how these strategic connections unlock a wealth of opportunities.

It's not just about receiving guidance but engaging in mutual exchanges where both mentor and mentee benefit, and where authentic networks open doors to professional and personal growth.

While the idea of mentorship and networking may seem daunting at first, these activities hold the potential to transform hesitation into opportunity.

Yet, these are activities that can transform an initial hesitation into great opportunities.

Are you ready to discover strategies that could redefine your professional journey?

Let's delve into the case for mentorship and uncover how it can unlock extraordinary opportunities for both personal and professional growth.

THE CASE FOR MENTORSHIP: FINDING YOUR GUIDING LIGHT

Have you ever wondered if mentorship could significantly influence your journey as an entrepreneur?

For those new to the business world, especially professionals over 50 looking to pivot, mentorship can serve as an invaluable resource.

Picture this: you're setting out in a field abundant with challenges and opportunities.

A mentor is like having a compass, guiding you to not only avoid pitfalls but also to recognize paths leading to success.

Unveiling the Benefits of Mentorship

Effective mentorship delivers a wealth of benefits, including personalized advice, seasoned wisdom, and strategic insights that dramatically accelerate your learning curve.

Consider Tom, who wanted to switch from corporate HR to launching his own consultancy.

With guidance from his mentor—a seasoned consultant—Tom mastered client acquisition through tailored strategies, bypassing years of trial and error.

Meet Steve, a retired teacher. He leveraged his passion for woodworking into an online shop.

Unsure how to generate leads and promote his work, Steve sought guidance from a local craft guild, where he found a mentor who helped him excel in the online marketplace.

In addition to tangible benefits, mentorship fosters confidence, broadens perspectives, and provides the crucial advantage of accountability.

A mentor provides encouragement and guidance, helping you push past limits as you start on your journey.

Identifying the Right Mentor

Finding the right mentor hinges on aligning with someone whose values and industry insights resonate with your ambitions.

Here are some actionable steps you can take to find and connect with your mentor:

Explore Professional Circles:

- Participate in industry events and workshops aligned with your interests to connect with experienced professionals.

- These environments are fertile grounds for building connections that might lead to mentorship.

Engage in Networking Events:

- Organizations often host networking programs tailored for entrepreneurs.

- Being actively involved not only expands your network but opens up possibilities for mentorship relationships.

Utilize LinkedIn:

- Use LinkedIn to identify and connect with potential mentors.

- When messaging, personalize your outreach by expressing genuine admiration for their work and explaining how their expertise aligns with your career goals.

Join Online Forums and Communities:

- Participating in groups focused on your area, like those on LinkedIn or Facebook, can introduce you to influential figures willing to share knowledge.

ACTION EXERCISE:

List three specific challenges you face in your career transition, and reflect on how a mentor's guidance could help you overcome them.

Think about how a mentor could help address these challenges.

Establishing a Mentorship Relationship

A successful mentor-mentee relationship is built on mutual respect, a genuine openness to learning, and active contributions from both parties.

After identifying potential mentors, initiate a conversation by introducing yourself and articulating your goals with clarity and purpose.

Help them understand what you're hoping to achieve in your business and in a potential mentoring relationship.

For professionals over 50, embracing mentorship can be a game-changer, significantly transforming your entrepreneurial journey.

The relationship can help you and your business grow faster and move smoothly in your journey, enabling you to accelerate your growth and transition smoothly into new ventures.

ACTION EXERCISE:

Identify three concrete steps you can take today to find and connect with a guiding mentor?

List 3 ways you can leverage your networks to create impactful and reciprocal relationships in your professional life.

Adding to the gift of mentorship...

As your mentor provides guidance and support, another avenue of opportunity often emerges: Networking.

Your mentor is likely involved in professional networks.

As your mentorship relationship grows, this often leads to more doors opening, including referrals to these potentially valuable networks.

As a result, you're introduced to wider circles of like-minded people.

Your wealth of experience can become a valuable asset in forging meaningful connections and unlocking new opportunities.

This can lead to potential collaborations and partnership opportunities that can help your business grow exponentially.

THE ART OF NETWORKING: UNLOCKING OPPORTUNITIES

Have you ever considered how success today often depends on who you know as much as what you know?

For professionals over 50 aiming to break into new fields might seem intimidating.

This is where strategically networking with successful professionals in your field can be extremely helpful.

By engaging with others in your field at network events and sharing your experiences and insights with peers and potential mentors...

It can open doors to opportunities, connections, and collaborations you might not have thought possible.

Remember: Every successful professional started with a first step—mentorship and networking can make yours easier.

Building Genuine Connections

Consider Jane, a retired professional who sought to turn her passion for food into a thriving local startup.

By attending industry-specific events and leveraging LinkedIn, Jane connected with key figures in the food industry.

These relationships helped her refine her concept and even secure startup advice from experts.

Take Mike, a retired engineer who successfully transitioned into tech consulting by tapping into his alumni network.

By reaching out to former classmates and colleagues, Mike tapped into a wealth of experience and connections that directed him toward freelance opportunities in tech.

These connections were instrumental in helping him navigate the latest industry trends.

This eventually led him to partnerships that enriched his consulting practice.

To create such genuine connections, focus on these actionable steps:

Attend Networking Events:

- Attend industry-specific meetups or conferences to connect with professionals who share your interests and expertise.

Utilize Online Platforms:

- LinkedIn isn't just for job hunting—use it to establish meaningful conversations.

- Join groups relevant to your industry and participate actively.

Engage in Professional Groups:

- Organizations often host group meetings or webinars, providing a platform to interact with other professionals and potential mentors who can provide insights and introductions.

Fostering Reciprocal Relationships

Networking is a two-way street: it's about giving as much as receiving.

Share your expertise, introduce connections, or volunteer your time for collaborations.

These actions foster trust and solidify professional bonds.

Martin, a former corporate sales professional, shared his expertise with a tech startup to refine their client outreach strategy.

His proactive contributions not only benefited the startup, but also opened the door to a consulting role that marked the beginning of an exciting new career chapter for him.

PRACTICAL STEPS TO GROW YOUR NETWORK

Here's how you can start building your network:

Map Out Potential Influencers:

- Identify individuals or leaders within your industry who could offer pivotal insights or connections.

Schedule Regular Follow-Ups:

- Good relationships need nurturing. Set reminders to check in with your contacts to build lasting connections.

Diversify Your Interactions:

- Engage with people from various fields to gain fresh perspectives and innovative ideas, essential for fostering creativity in your work.

Ultimately, the strength of your network lies in the depth of your connections.

Building a strong network requires consistent effort and reflection.

As you take these practical steps, consider how you can integrate them into your daily professional life.

REFLECTIVE QUESTIONS:

What steps will you take today to nurture and expand your professional network?

What specific skills or experiences can you share with a mentor?

Which skills would you like a mentor to help you develop?

With the groundwork of mentorship and a robust network, you set the stage for transformative personal and professional growth.

But how do these relationships come to life in real-world success stories?

Let's expand on what you heard about in the introduction, with more inspiring narratives that bring the concepts of strategic networking and mentorship to life, showcasing how they unlock doors and foster mutually beneficial relationships.

STORIES THAT INSPIRE: A JOURNEY TO NEW BEGINNINGS

In the world of entrepreneurship, the right guidance and connections can truly redefine your path.

These real-world success stories highlight how strategic mentorship and meaningful connections can transform careers.

From entrepreneurs finding guidance to professionals discovering opportunities through shared insights, these narratives demonstrate the tangible impact of networking

Mentorship in Action: Oprah Winfrey and Maya Angelou

Oprah Winfrey credits much of her personal and professional growth to the mentorship of Maya Angelou, whom she met during a pivotal career moment in the 1980s.

Angelou's wisdom on understanding one's identity and values deeply influenced Windrey.

A standout piece of advice, 'When you learn, teach. When you get, give,' became a guiding principle in Winfrey's media and philanthropic endeavors.

This guidance was evident when Winfrey introduced "The Oprah Winfrey Show" with a focus on self-help, literature, and spirituality, directly inspired by Angelou's teachings.

Winfrey's subsequent endeavors, from founding the Leadership Academy for Girls in South Africa to producing meaningful content on her network OWN, reflect the lasting impact of Angelou's mentorship.

Their relationship demonstrated how a mentor could not only influence career choices but also inspire a legacy of giving back to the community and empowering others.

While Oprah's story illustrates the profound impact of mentorship at the pinnacle of success, mentorship can also transform lives at any stage of a career.

Real-World Networking: Donna's Journey to Success

At 55, Donna made the bold decision to leave her corporate career to follow her passion for organic gardening.

The journey was thrilling, but filled with challenges, particularly in crafting a market strategy and positioning the products.

Everything changed when she attended a sustainable agriculture seminar and met Sarah, a seasoned expert in the field.

Sarah offered practical advice on crafting a unique selling proposition centered around eco-friendly packaging, which differentiated Donna's products in a crowded marketplace.

Moreover, with Sarah's encouragement, Donna participated in local farmers' markets, gaining firsthand customer feedback and iterating her products based on community needs.

Inspired by her mentor's holistic approach, she also introduced educational workshops on organic gardening, which became a hit and increased her brand's visibility.

Through her network, Donna secured a partnership with a local store, boosting her sales significantly. Her journey epitomizes how mentorship coupled with strategic networking can transform dreams into tangible success stories, even in the face of late-career changes.

These stories reflect the limitless possibilities unlocked through strategic mentorship and networking, proving that the right relationships can set the stage for groundbreaking career transformations.

Which narrative resonates with your own professional journey?

As we consider using mentorship and networking to take our professional and personal lives to the next level, let's review and highlight the key takeaways that can empower you to build and sustain these transformative relationships in your own journey.

KEY TAKEAWAYS

As you've now become keenly aware, unlocking the full potential of mentorship and networking can significantly propel your personal and professional growth.

Here are the key takeaways from this chapter to guide you on your journey:

Seek Strategic Mentorship:

Connect with mentors who share your values and possess expertise relevant to your goals.

Platforms like LinkedIn and industry events are excellent tools for finding mentors who can provide meaningful guidance and support.

Build Meaningful Networks:

Engage with professional groups and attend events to create genuine connections.

Focus on building relationships that offer mutual benefits and open doors to new opportunities.

Embrace Reciprocal Relationships:

Successful mentorship and networking relationships are built on reciprocity.

Offer your insights and support to others, and be open to receiving their help in return, fostering a community of shared growth.

Leverage Both Online and Offline Opportunities:

Take advantage of digital tools and platforms to enhance your reach and connections, while also utilizing in-person gatherings that reinforce bonds.

Adapt and Grow Through Networking:

Use your network to gain new perspectives and innovate within your field.

Stay open to learning and expanding your knowledge through the diverse insights offered by your connections.

Mentorship and networking are your keys to unlocking extraordinary growth and success in both your personal and professional life.

By cultivating these connections, you create a cycle of mutual giving and receiving, paving the way for enduring achievements.

Now, let's wrap up by examining how these practices can leave a lasting, fulfilling impact on your life.

CONCLUSION: THE POWER OF CONNECTION AND GROWTH

Mentorship and networking have the transformative power to elevate both your career and your personal life in meaningful, lasting ways.

Together, mentorship and networking form the foundation of a fulfilling second act, empowering you to step confidently into new ventures.

We've explored how these strategic relationships open doors to opportunities that might otherwise remain hidden, providing both guidance and a means to achieve your aspirations.

The stories of Oprah Winfrey and Donna remind us of the enduring power of mentorship and networking.

Oprah, guided by Maya Angelou, learned invaluable lessons of resilience and authenticity that propelled her into the influential figure she is today.

Similarly, Donna's journey from corporate life to successful entrepreneurship was guided by the support of her mentor and the power of community networking, allowing her to navigate her transition with confidence and ease.

These stories highlight the mutual rewards of mentorship, where shared wisdom is enriched by fresh perspectives and renewed passion.

As you consider the role of mentorship and networking in your own path, remember that these practices not only unlock opportunities but also foster a fulfilling cycle of growth and contribution.

Embrace the power of these relationships to shape your journey.

By seeking out mentors who inspire and challenge you, and by actively participating in networks that resonate with your goals, you lay the groundwork for sustainable success and personal fulfillment.

As you continue this journey, let the connections you build light your way and help you to not only reach your goals, but inspire others along the way.

ACTION EXERCISE:

Take the initiative to identify one networking event or group to attend this month.

Set a clear goal to establish meaningful connections.

Next, while you're building impactful connections through mentorship and networking, it's just as important to keep your personal and professional worlds in balance and harmony.

As we move to the next chapter, we'll explore how you can work toward achieving work-life balance, so you can keep moving forward, thriving while sustaining your newfound growth and inspiration.

CHAPTER 13

ACHIEVING WORK-LIFE BALANCE:

INTRODUCTION: FINDING HARMONY IN THE HUSTLE

Imagine this: It's 9 pm, and your email notifications won't stop buzzing.

You're torn between finishing a work task and spending time with your loved ones.

Does this sound familiar?

If you've ever felt pulled in a dozen directions at once, you're not alone.

The pressure to juggle it all—especially later in life—can feel overwhelming.

The good news is that balance is possible—and your journey toward it begins right here.

Think about a moment when everything seemed urgent.

You were being pulled in multiple directions at once: work deadlines, family, partner, friends, and your own health and stress level...

If you were able to put all of your responsibilities and activities into balance at that moment, how would that have shifted the outcome—not just for your career, but for your peace of mind?

Consider the transformative journey of Arianna Huffington's as a compelling example.

As the co-founder of The Huffington Post, Arianna experienced the intense pressures of growing a media empire firsthand.

The breaking point came when the toll of sleepless nights and constant pressure led to a collapse from sheer exhaustion, resulting in a broken cheekbone.

This wasn't just a physical crash; it was a wake-up call that forced her to rethink her priorities.

This turning point drove Arianna to prioritize balance in her life, focusing on well-being and health over relentless ambition.

She became an outspoken advocate for work-life balance, emphasizing the power of sleep, mindfulness, and stress management.

Her book, "Thrive," plays with the idea of redefining success to include well-being, wisdom, and wonder, extending beyond just professional milestones.

Arianna's story is a powerful reminder of the need for balance, even in the high-stakes world of entrepreneurship.

Her transformation shows us that by reshaping our personal and professional priorities, we can achieve a fulfilling and enriched life that guards against burnout and supports long-term happiness.

Now, let's turn to Jane, a 55-year-old professional who transitioned from a long corporate career to pursuing her passion by opening a small art gallery.

Initially, Jane found herself overwhelmed, trying to handle everything from logistics to marketing. Her health and personal life began to suffer as a result.

Recognizing the unsustainable pace, Jane decided to apply principles of work-life balance that she had once set aside.

She implemented structured work hours, adopting mindfulness practices, and delegated tasks that didn't require her personal involvement.

By setting firm boundaries for work and personal time, Jane achieved a notable improvement in her business.

Over the course of a year, she experienced a 30% increase in productivity and a significant boost in client satisfaction.

Personally, she found increased fulfillment by having more dedicated time with family, which enriched her relationships and added to her sense of joy and purpose.

Jane's story underscores that regardless of age or career stage, deliberate and mindful adjustments to priorities can foster better work-life balance and a more fulfilling personal and professional life.

Now, let's discover some strategies tailored to help you find this balance, too.

We'll explore how finding improved balance can propel you towards a more sustainable, successful path.

DEFINING WORK-LIFE BALANCE: FINDING YOUR UNIQUE RHYTHM

Have you ever heard the term 'work-life harmony'?

This concept emphasizes a fluid integration of personal and professional life, rather than suggesting an equal division of time.

Both concepts of work-life balance and work-life harmony aim to help us blend work with our personal lives in ways that reflect what truly matters to us.

So, how can you integrate your personal values into your definition of success?

Work-life balance doesn't necessarily mean dividing your time equally between work and personal life.

For some, it might mean flexible hours that allow for midday yoga, while for others, it might be an evening set aside for family time.

The key is recognizing that balance—whether called balance or harmony—looks different for everyone.

Consider Emily, who left her corporate job in her early 50s to launch her own consulting firm.

Seeking greater flexibility, she aimed to balance her career with her love for travel and personal projects.

By clearly defining her personal and professional goals, Emily was able to create a business model that supported both her livelihood and her dreams.

Her journey transformed the usual hustle into a fulfilling lifestyle.

Incorporating balance can significantly enhance various aspects of our lives.

It boosts productivity, as time away from work provides mental clarity and renewal.

It fuels creativity by generating space for new ideas and perspectives.

Most importantly, it leads to personal fulfillment, as you align your actions with what truly brings you joy and purpose.

Consider John, a 58-year-old who transitioned from a demanding office job to teach part-time at a local college.

By realigning his work to match his passion for mentoring young students, John found renewed energy and satisfaction, illustrating the profound personal growth that comes from aligning professional life with personal values.

Remember, achieving work-life balance isn't about rigidly dividing time but about creating a lifestyle that truly reflects your values and aspirations.

Embrace the challenge of weaving your personal values into your professional life, and discover how fulfilling that journey can be.

Now that we've established what work-life balance looks like, let's explore practical strategies to incorporate this balance into your entrepreneurial life.

By setting clear boundaries and making personal well-being a priority, you can achieve a harmonious blend of professional success and personal fulfillment.

Let's look at the core strategies that will help you stay balanced as you pursue your ambitious goals.

CORE STRATEGIES FOR WORK-LIFE BALANCE

SETTING BOUNDARIES: CLAIMING YOUR TIME

Imagine you're enjoying dinner with your family, but work keeps interrupting.

Setting firm boundaries can be your shield against such intrusions.

Identify your non-negotiables—activities or time slots that you prioritize without exception, such as family dinners or morning walks.

Think of Sarah, a small business owner over 50, who decided her Sundays were family-only days.

By communicating these boundaries clearly with her clients and herself, she preserved precious time for personal rejuvenation.

TIME MANAGEMENT: THE POWER OF PRIORITIZATION

Effective time management is like having an extra set of hands.

Take the Eisenhower Matrix—a favorite among busy professionals.

Consider Mark, a dedicated father and aspiring entrepreneur, skillfully used the Eisenhower Matrix to keep his priorities in check.

Juggling the demands of building his side hustle, a full-time job, family responsibilities, and personal relaxation seemed overwhelming.

However, by categorizing tasks using the Eisenhower Matrix, he avoided burnout, and progressively built his side hustle without sacrificing family time.

EISENHOWER MATRIX		
	HIGH URGENCY	LOW URGENCY
HIGH IMPORTANCE	IMPORTANT & URGENT. Tasks with clear deadlines and important consequences if immediate action is not taken.	IMPORTANT, NOT URGENT. Tasks without a deadline, but remain important to complete.
LOW IMPORTANCE	URGENT, but NOT IMPORTANT. Tasks that need to be done, but are not high on your priority list. Can be delegated to others.	NOT IMPORTANT, NOT URGENT. Tasks that are not important and can be delayed or deleted.

The Eisenhower Matrix is a practical that helps prioritize tasks by dividing them into four categories:

Urgent and Important:

Tasks in this category require your immediate attention and are crucial to achieving your immediate goals. This often includes deadlines, pressing problems, or critical meetings.

Important, Not Urgent:

These are activities that help you reach long-term goals. They require thoughtful planning but aren't pressing. This includes strategic planning, education, and relationship-building tasks.

Urgent, Not Important:

These tasks demand immediate reaction but are not linked to your long-term objectives. Delegating these tasks, such as certain emails or calls, can allow you to focus on more significant activities.

Not Urgent, Not Important:

These tasks are often distractions that neither help achieve your short-term nor long-term goals. They can typically be minimized or eliminated as they contribute little to your productivity.

Here's how Mark categorized his tasks :

1. Urgent and Important: Mark prioritized attending his children's school events and handling daily work responsibilities, ensuring neither was overlooked.

2. Important, Not Urgent: He dedicated evenings for long-term planning and strategizing for his online business, setting weekly goals and tracking progress.

3. Urgent, Not Important: Household chores and routine shopping were delegated to family members or handled through delivery services, freeing up time without neglecting essential tasks.

4. Not Urgent, Not Important: Mark consciously avoided unnecessary distractions such as excessive

television or unproductive online browsing, focusing instead on tasks that aligned with his family and business goals.

By clearly distinguishing his priorities, Mark maintained active involvement with his children while steadily building his business, achieving a fulfilling and balanced life."

Here's how you can use it:

1. List Your Tasks: Begin by writing down all the tasks you need to complete.

2. Categorize: Use the Eisenhower Matrix to sort tasks into four quadrants:

- Urgent and Important: Do these tasks immediately.

- Important, Not Urgent: Schedule time to focus on these.

- Urgent, Not Important: Delegate if possible.

- Not Urgent, Not Important: Minimize or eliminate tasks that don't contribute to your goals.

Plan:

Commit to tackling tasks in the right order, freeing both your mind and time for what truly matters.

PRIORITIZING WELL-BEING: NURTURE YOUR MIND AND BODY

In the midst of work, never forget the importance of self-care.

Regular physical activity, like a brisk walk or yoga, replenishes your energy.

Add mindfulness practices like meditation or journaling to keep your mind sharp and stress-free.

In her 50s, Jane found solace in daily meditation, which not only boosted her mood but also sparked creative ideas for her home-based business.

DELEGATION AND AUTOMATION: SMART WORK, NOT HARD WORK

Leverage technology and smart outsourcing to work more efficiently.

Tools like automation software can handle repetitive tasks, freeing you to focus on growth areas.

Similarly, platforms like Upwork can connect you with freelancers for tasks like design or content writing.

Linda, a professional managing both a family and a side business, used these tools to streamline her workload, giving her more time for her loved ones.

By setting boundaries and embracing time management, we not only make room for our professional ambitions but also create space for personal rejuvenation.

WORK-LIFE BALANCE EXERCISE:

Identify the activities or commitments that are most important in both your personal and professional life. (These are your non-negotiables).

List three activities that leave you feeling refreshed and energized (e.g. hobbies, exercise, family time)

Develop a plan to ensure these activities have a place in your daily or weekly schedule.

Consider using tools like Trello or a Calendar to set reminders and block out time specifically for these recharging activities.

Remember, it's all about finding what works uniquely for you and leaning into it with intention.

However, even with these strategies in place, burnout can still creep in unexpectedly.

Let's explore how to identify and prevent burnout, ensuring that the quest for harmony supports both your well-being and entrepreneurial success.

RECOGNIZING AND PREVENTING BURNOUT: GUARDING YOUR ENERGY

Have you ever felt like the passion that once fueled your entrepreneurial dreams is now consuming you?

This could be burnout, a state of physical, emotional, and mental exhaustion caused by prolonged stress.

It creeps in when you're continuously overwhelmed, leading to symptoms such as chronic fatigue, irritability, lack of motivation, and difficulty concentrating.

Consider Carol, who at age 52 decided to leave her corporate job and start an online consulting business.

Despite her enthusiasm, she began to notice signs of burn-out within months.

She was always tired, lost her drive, and felt disconnected from her passion.

Identifying these symptoms early, Carol took proactive steps to reclaim her well-being.

SIGNS OF BURNOUT

Chronic Fatigue:

- Feeling persistently drained and struggling to find energy.

Irritability:

- Becoming easily frustrated with yourself or others, even over minor issues.

Reduced Performance:

- Struggling to concentrate and complete tasks effectively.

Disinterest in work:

- Experiencing a loss of enthusiasm or motivation for the work you once loved.

ADDRESSING BURNOUT PROACTIVELY

Awareness and Reflection:

Regularly check in with yourself to identify signs of stress or fatigue.

Ask questions like, "How am I feeling emotionally and physically?"

Establish Routines:

Create a daily schedule that includes breaks and personal time.

Carol found relief by setting clear work hours and unwinding with a relaxing hobby at the end of her day.

Seek Support:

Sharing challenges with peers or mentors can offer relief and fresh perspectives.

Engage with communities that inspire and motivate you.

Pursue Passion Projects:

Dedicate time to activities you love, which help revitalize your energy and enthusiasm.

RECOVERY FROM BURNOUT

Take the story of Alex who, at 58, found himself burned out while juggling a side gig and a full-time job.

Alex overcame his burnout by making intentional, manageable changes to his routine.

By committing to consistent sleep and adopting a morning meditation practice, he gradually restored his energy.

This approach not only improved his mood but also led to a significant revival in his creative thinking, which was crucial for his side gig.

These small changes added up to improve his overall work performance and personal satisfaction.

Alex's journey shows that with thoughtful adjustments and attention to self-care, overcoming burnout is within reach.

Burnout doesn't have to be the end of your journey.

By recognizing its signs and taking deliberate actions, you can nurture resilience and regain the joy that first inspired your entrepreneurial journey.

Here are some strategies to consider if you find yourself on the edge of being burned out:

Rest and Recharge:

- Prioritize adequate rest and sleep to restore your energy.

Professional Help:

- Consider professional counseling or coaching for personalized strategies.

Incremental Changes:

- Make small, manageable lifestyle changes instead of drastic shifts.

Let's see how these principles unfold in everyday entrepreneurial life.

By looking at real-world examples, we can witness the art of balancing aspirations with personal well-being, illustrating how these concepts are put into practice to achieve a harmonious life.

While proactive strategies are essential, recognizing and addressing burnout ensures you stay on track toward a balanced life.

APPLYING LESSONS LEARNED

In the world of entrepreneurship, real and illustrative examples bring strategies to life, providing concrete lessons we can apply to our own journeys.

Let's explore a combination of fictional scenarios and a real-life story to see how individuals have successfully balanced their professional ambitions with personal well-being.

BUILDING BALANCE AMIDST GROWTH: LISA

Meet Lisa, a 55-year-old entrepreneur who founded a sustainable fashion startup.

At first, juggling her business and family commitments felt overwhelming.

She implemented a strategy of setting firm work-life boundaries—designating evenings for family and weekends technology-free.

This routine allowed her to recharge while maintaining business momentum.

Her takeaway? Maintaining consistent boundaries leads to greater personal satisfaction and stronger business focus.

HARMONIZING ROLES WITH PASSION: BRIAN

Consider Brian, a 60-year-old restaurateur who opened a small eatery focusing on organic foods.

To balance the demands of his restaurant with his passion for cycling, Brian scheduled rides during the quiet hours before the lunch shift.

By integrating his passion for cycling into his daily routine, Brian not only alleviated stress but also saw a 20% increase in customer satisfaction.

He credited the improvement to the creative menu ideas inspired during his rides.

This strategic scheduling allowed him to maintain energy and enthusiasm, leading to a more engaging dining experience for his patrons.

It also provided for greater personal satisfaction in balancing his professional commitments with his personal interests.

The lesson? Harmonizing work with personal interests can enhance both productivity and happiness.

CREATING PHYSICAL AND MENTAL BOUNDARIES: SARAH

According to Jobera.com, research shows that employers have observed high retention and productivity rates from workers who take regular breaks. And these employees are 80% less likely to quit due to high job satisfaction.

Research on lunch breaks shows that 40% of employees reported feeling less stressed after taking lunch breaks and

37% reported feeling less burnt out after eating and relaxing during a break.

For Sarah, a freelance graphic designer in her 50s, working from home presented unique challenges.

To avoid mixing work and leisure, Sarah created a distinct workspace and scheduled regular breaks.

By setting clear physical and mental boundaries—such as a dedicated workspace and regular breaks—Sarah experienced higher work satisfaction and boosted productivity.

These structured breaks not only reduced stress but also led to a 35% boost in her creative output.

With this approach, Sarah found it easier to disconnect from work at the end of the day, leading to a healthier work-life balance and improved overall well-being.

This echoed findings that emphasize the importance of regular breaks for maintaining high job satisfaction and reduced burnout.

Sarah's experience highlights the importance of creating physical and mental boundaries in a home working environment to sustain enthusiasm and efficiency.

REAL-LIFE INSPIRATION: SHERYL SANDBERG

Sheryl Sandberg, COO of Facebook and author of Lean In, has openly discussed the challenges of balancing a high-powered career with personal life.

After experiencing personal loss and the pressures of her role, Sandberg emphasized the importance of setting clear boundaries and prioritizing self-care.

She implemented strategies such as leaving work at a reasonable hour to have dinner with her children and ensuring weekends were largely dedicated to family.

Sandberg also openly communicates with her boundaries with her team, helping manage expectations and sustain focus and efficiency at work.

Her story highlights the importance of setting priorities and being transparent about personal needs to maintain balance amid demanding professional responsibilities.

Through these stories, we learn that personalizing our approach to balance—combining strategic planning with personal passions—empowers us to maintain harmony and sustain success in entrepreneurship.

ACTION EXERCISE:

Take a moment to write down three tasks you can delegate this week.

What tools or people could help take on these tasks and lighten your load?

How will this help improve both your personal and professional life?

Are you ready to take action?

By learning the strategies that have successfully balanced personal and professional lives, it becomes clear that achieving harmony amid ambition is not only possible but essential.

Let's now summarize the key strategies that can help you cultivate a seamless balance between success and wellbeing on your own journey.

KEY TAKEAWAYS

As we've navigated the path to achieving work-life balance, the importance of these strategies becomes undeniably clear.

Each takeaway represents a powerful tool that not only enhances your professional endeavors but also enriches your personal life.

By embracing these practices, you're not just optimizing your work routine—you're cultivating a lifestyle that prioritizes harmony, fulfillment, and sustained success.

Let's revisit these essential lessons that can transform both your entrepreneurial journey and your personal well-being.

Establish Clear Boundaries:

- Define non-negotiables, such as family time and personal hobbies, to maintain a healthy separation between work and personal life.

Master Time Management:

- Use techniques like the Pomodoro Technique and Eisenhower Matrix to prioritize tasks effectively and reduce stress.

Prioritize Well-Being:

- Make mindfulness, regular exercise, and self-care part of your routine to nurture both mental and physical health.

Leverage Delegation and Automation:

- Leverage technology and outsourcing to manage tasks efficiently, freeing up time for strategic thinking and personal pursuits.

Recognize and Prevent Burnout:

- Stay alert to signs of burnout and take proactive steps, such as seeking support and scheduling regular downtime, to recover.

Personalize Your Balance:

- Remember, work-life harmony is unique to each person. Align your strategies with your values and personal circumstances.

By adopting these key strategies, you'll create a fulfilling balance, where entrepreneurial success and personal happiness coexist harmoniously.

Equipped with these essential insights, you're now poised to integrate work-life balance into your entrepreneurial pursuits, creating a life where success and personal well-being go hand in hand.

As we conclude this chapter, let's reflect on the journey towards seamless coexistence of our ambitions and personal harmony.

CONCLUSION AND SEGUE: EMBRACING THE HARMONY OF SUCCESS

Let's reflect on the profound journey of achieving work-life balance.

We've learned that at the core of entrepreneurship is not just the pursuit of financial success but also the quest for a harmonious life where professional accomplishments and personal well-being coexist seamlessly.

From Lisa's determination to maintain family nights reserved for her closest ones, to Sheryl Sandberg's public advocacy for clear boundaries and self-care, each story serves as a reminder that balance is achievable with thoughtful intention.

This chapter underscores that true success in entrepreneurship extends beyond financial gains to include achieving a balanced and fulfilling personal life, as well.

It's evident that setting boundaries and prioritizing personal well-being alongside business goals are not just beneficial—they're essential.

For those finding it challenging to separate work from personal life, remember that creating boundaries is an ongoing practice.

Achieving balance isn't about perfection. It's about progress.

Every small step you take toward harmony will bring lasting benefits to both your personal and professional life.

Seek mentors who have walked this path before you and explore networking opportunities that offer support and guidance.

Surrounding yourself with like-minded individuals can provide both inspiration and practical advice, helping you set boundaries and priorities while cultivating a thriving lifestyle and vibrant business.

Ask yourself, 'What advice would you offer an entrepreneur struggling to set boundaries?'

Perhaps it's the reminder that sustainable success is a marathon, not a sprint, and that taking care of yourself is the first step toward achieving your goals.

As we move forward, remember that balancing work and life as an entrepreneur is not just an aspirational goal—it's a fundamental strategy for long-term success.

By embracing the principles of work-life balance, you can thrive professionally while living a life that aligns with your values.

Let this knowledge guide you in crafting a life that honors both your aspirations and your inner peace.

Now, let's look ahead to the next chapter, where we explore the art of storytelling and its power to deepen connections and expand your entrepreneurial reach.

CHAPTER 14

SHARING YOUR JOURNEY

INTRODUCTION: CRAFTING CONNECTIONS THROUGH STORYTELLING

Have you ever wondered how a simple story could spark a movement?

Let's begin with Blake Mycoskie, the founder of TOMS Shoes, whose journey in Argentina inspired an idea that not only transformed his business, but also changed the lives of countless children worldwide.

By witnessing the struggles of children without shoes, Blake didn't just start a footwear company—he launched a global movement through the 'One for One' model, where each purchase directly helps a child in need.

Blake didn't just create products; he wove narratives that allowed customers to participate in a shared mission, fostering an emotional connection that transcends ordinary transactions.

Just as Blake Mycoskie harnessed the power of story-driven collaboration with his 'One for One' model, Patagonia shows how aligning business strategies with environmental commitment can create a strong bond with customers.

Through their "Worn Wear" campaign, Patagonia encouraged customers to engage deeply with the brand's mission of sustainability.

Through campaigns like 'Worn Wear,' Patagonia shares stories that promote repair and reuse, weaving sustainability into its brand narrative.

These stories not only promote their products but also invite customers to join a broader cause of environmental stewardship.

Both Blake's and Patagonia's stories illustrate how storytelling can drive transformative connections and growth.

Now, imagine an entrepreneur in their fifties who turned a personal hardship into a thriving business.

Meet Linda, a professional in her fifties who transformed a career shift into a thriving side business by crafting herbal teas for stress relief.

Facing initial challenges like financial constraints and industry inexperience, Linda used her personal journey to build her brand.

Her story resonated deeply with a community seeking natural wellness solutions.

Through local workshops and authentic storytelling, her business not only gained traction but also built a supportive network of wellness enthusiasts.

Linda's journey shows how aligning personal passions with business can drive both personal success and community wellbeing.

Her story offers an inspiring model for those looking to start anew later in life.

This chapter explores storytelling as a powerful tool for entrepreneurs.

Whether you're scaling a startup or reinventing your career, the stories you craft can forge lasting connections, inspire action, and foster both personal and business growth.

REFLECTIVE QUESTION:

Think about your entrepreneurial journey: What personal experiences can you share in a story that will inspire others?

As we journey through these narratives, you'll discover how to transform challenges into compelling stories that captivate and connect.

Ready to explore this narrative art? Let's begin.

WHY STORYTELLING MATTERS

Think about your favorite brand—it's likely not just their products you recall, but the compelling stories they share.

Chances are, it's not just the products you remember, but the stories they tell. Storytelling is a vital tool that goes beyond mere marketing—it's a bridge that connects, inspires, and transforms relationships.

Research reveals that 92% of consumers prefer ads that feel like stories, and effective storytelling can boost purchases by up to 30%.

When consumers genuinely connect with a brand's story, 15% are inspired to make an immediate purchase.

Why does storytelling have such an impact?

Building Emotional Bridges:

Storytelling forges genuine connections by evoking emotions and tapping into shared experiences that deeply resonate with audiences.

When a brand successfully taps into these personal stories, it transcends mere transactions, building trust far beyond what conventional marketing can achieve.

This trust acts as a foundation for lasting customer loyalty, where individuals transition from being passive consumers to passionate advocates of the brand's underlying mission.

By weaving emotional connections through storytelling, businesses turn their customers into dedicated, loyal supporters who feel a genuine part of the brand's journey and success.

Inspiring Action and Fostering Loyalty:

A compelling narrative has the power to transform passive observers into active participants.

When people feel part of a brand's story, they become invested in its success, leading to increased engagement, advocacy, and even personal transformation.

For instance, a brand that effectively tells its story doesn't need to push products aggressively; instead, customers are drawn to buy into the lifestyle or mission that the brand represents.

Transforming Products into Purpose:

Imagine a small bakery that initially seemed to offer nothing more than fresh bread.

By weaving a meaningful mission into its story, such as partnering with local farmers for organic grains and sharing surplus with nearby shelters, this bakery redefines itself as a community-focused endeavor.

Customers aren't simply purchasing bread; they're contributing to a meaningful cause that aligns with their values.

This shift effectively transforms a routine purchase into a supportive action.

This small change shows how ordinary products can evolve into powerful, mission-driven offerings that engage and inspire community involvement.

A Path to Personal Growth:

Storytelling isn't solely for building brands; it's a profound tool for fostering personal growth and resilience.

Crafting and telling one's story allows individuals to reflect on their journeys, acknowledge challenges, and celebrate achievements.

This self-reflection fosters adaptability and perseverance, essential components for any entrepreneur.

In conclusion, storytelling shapes brands and lives.

By integrating your mission into a compelling narrative, you cultivate a loyal community while inspiring both personal and collective growth.

As we begin to see the immense power storytelling holds in weaving connections and inspiring growth, it becomes crucial to understand what makes a story truly compelling.

Let's delve into these essential components to craft stories that resonate deeply and build enduring connections with your community.

Ready to craft your story?

CORE ELEMENTS OF A COMPELLING STORY

A story is far more than a mere sequence of events; it's a dynamic narrative that has the power to inspire your audience, ignite change, and forge lasting connections.

To craft a story that truly captivates, consider these core elements:

AUTHENTICITY

Authenticity is the cornerstone of effective storytelling.

It involves sharing honest experiences and authentic perspectives that define your brand.

Customers can often sense when stories feel artificial, so staying true to your brand's values and mission is vital.

For example, Patagonia's dedication to environmental stewardship is evident in campaigns like 'Worn Wear,' which encourage customers to repair and reuse their gear, perfectly aligning practices with advocacy.

RELATABILITY

A story truly resonates when your audience can see themselves in it.

Relatable stories bridge the divide between your brand and its audience by reflecting shared experiences and aspirations.

For instance, a homegrown startup sharing the growing pains of breaking into a market may connect with aspiring entrepreneurs facing similar struggles.

CONFLICT AND RESOLUTION

Every compelling narrative contains a conflict or challenge followed by a resolution.

This narrative structure captivates your audience while showcasing your brand's resilience and problem-solving abilities.

Consider Blake Mycoskie's TOMS Shoes: the initial problem was a lack of shoes for children in Argentina, and the resolution was the innovative "One for One" model.

Stories like these illustrate the brand's commitment to making a difference.

STORYTELLING FRAMEWORK

To effectively tell your brand's story, follow this three-part framework:

The Challenge:

- Highlight a meaningful obstacle that your brand has encountered.

- Example: A startup struggling with gaining visibility in a saturated market.

The Resolution:

- Share how you overcame this challenge.

- Example: They leveraged unique social media campaigns to highlight their distinctive product features.

The Emotional or Inspirational Impact:

- Illustrate the impact or emotion that resulted from this journey.

- Example: The campaign not only increased sales but also built a community of supportive and engaged customers who advocate for the brand.

IMPLEMENTING STORYTELLING EFFECTIVELY

Start with Your Purpose:

- Clearly articulate why your brand exists and the core values that inspire it.

Identify Your Audience:

- Tailor your stories to reflect the interests and challenges of your target audience.

Be Concise Yet Evocative:

- Craft stories that are easy to understand but rich in emotion.

Use Multiple Platforms:

- Share your stories across diverse platforms to reach a wider audience.

Foster Engagement:

- Invite your audience to share their personal experiences with your brand, deepening the connection.

Incorporating these elements into your storytelling strategy not only enhances your brand's narrative but also fosters a deep-seated connection with your audience.

By embracing authenticity, relatability, conflict, and resolution, your stories can inspire action and build lasting belief in your brand.

Understanding the core elements that make a story impactful is only the beginning.

REFLECTIVE QUESTION:

Reflect on a personal story that showcases your resilience or unveils your 'Why'—the deeper purpose behind choosing your business niche.

How can you share this with your audience?

The next step is to choose the right platforms to share these narratives, amplifying your message and reaching your community where they are most engaged.

By strategically selecting these platforms, you can enhance your brand's presence and reinforce connections, turning stories into bridges that unite your audience around shared values and experiences.

Let's explore how you can leverage different media to tell your story effectively.

PLATFORMS FOR STORYTELLING

Today's digital landscape offers a wide variety of platforms for sharing your stories.

Start small and see where your creativity takes you.

These channels are not just for broadcasting your narrative; they invite you to engage with your audience in dynamic, interactive ways.

Let's take a look at a few of these platforms and explore them together.

Blogging

Blogging provides a space to delve into in-depth narratives. Don't worry about perfection; begin with a straightforward story about a business lesson and why it matters to you.

- Introduction: Share the core of your lesson and explain why it resonates with you?

- The Challenge: Talk about the problem you faced. Simple, relatable details will draw readers in.

- The Resolution: Explain how you turned things around, shedding light on your decisions.

- Key Takeaways: Wrap up with what you learned. How can this help someone else?

For added connection, use pictures and personal stories.

Don't shy away from inviting readers to engage with thoughts or questions.

Social Media

Platforms like Instagram, X, and Facebook are not just for posting; they're spaces to share quick, personal stories.

Here are a few creative ideas:

1. A photo detailing a daily challenge you faced and conquered.

2. A short video showing a personal or professional win.

3. A #Throwback post sharing past hurdles and growth.

4. A poll asking folks about their challenges.

5. A meaningful quote or lesson that resonates with you.

Remember, using tags can broaden your reach. The conversations with your audience in the comments are genuinely valuable.

Video and Vlogging:

Videos add a vibrant, dynamic dimension to storytelling. Get comfortable and draft a simple script:

- Opening: Say hello! Share who you are and what you're about.

- The Spark: What sparked the idea for your brand?

- The Path: Highlight any challenges and standout moments.

- Core Values: Reinforce what truly drives your business.

- Closing Note: Invite viewers to connect further with you.

Stay true to yourself on camera. High-quality video and audio can help, but they needn't be perfect.

Podcasting:

Podcasts provide an intimate medium for investigating stories in depth, offering opportunities to explore themes such as failure and growth.

- Introduction: What's this episode about?

- First Lesson: Describe a failure that taught you something essential.

- Second Lesson: Share another story, focusing on growth.

- Third Lesson: End with a transformative tale of change.

- Conclusion: Reflect. How do these stories shape your path?

An inviting tone and vivid language resonate deeply with audiences. Bringing in guests can provide fresh perspectives and inspiring insights.

These platforms are not merely channels; they are stages for storytelling that humanize your brand, foster engagement, and build lasting connections with your audience.

Your storytelling on these platforms doesn't need to be perfect from the beginning.

However, it's important that your stories remain authentic and impactful, reinforcing the connections that your brand seeks to build.

Start small, and let each new post or episode build your confidence.

Enjoy experimentation and connect with others by sharing the power of your stories. As you continue to share your stories and experiment with various approaches, it's natural to encounter challenges along the way.

The good news is that every obstacle comes with strategies to navigate and overcome it.

Let's dive into some practical tools and insights to help ensure your storytelling remains impactful and connects deeply with your audience.

OVERCOMING CHALLENGES IN STORYTELLING

While storytelling can be a powerful tool for entrepreneurs, it is not without its challenges.

Finding the right balance between authenticity and promotion, maintaining a consistent tone, and aligning your narratives with your brand can all be daunting tasks.

Let's explore some strategies to help navigate these common hurdles.

MAINTAINING AUTHENTICITY

Authenticity is vital in storytelling, yet it's easier to falter when striving to project an ideal image. Here's how you can ensure your stories stay sincere:

- Stay True to Your Values: Develop narratives that reflect your core mission and values, as consistency in messaging builds trust.

- Engage Honestly: Share both successes and setbacks. Transparency builds credibility.

- Reflect Real Experiences: Use real-life anecdotes and examples to highlight genuine experiences.

Tip: Balance transparency with brand alignment by clearly defining what your brand stands for and ensuring that all narratives are consistent with these principles.

FINDING THE RIGHT TONE

The tone of your stories should resonate with your audience and reflect your brand's personality.

Consider these tips:

Know Your Audience:

- Identify the language and style that will resonate most with your target audience.

Stay Consistent:

- Maintain a tone that aligns with your brand across all platforms to establish a recognizable voice.

Adapt When Necessary:

- Be flexible and willing to adjust the tone based on the context or platform without losing the essence of your brand.

BALANCING PROMOTION AND NARRATIVE

While promotion is essential, it should not overshadow the authenticity of your narrative.

Here are some strategies to maintain this balance:

Focus on the Story First:

- Start with a narrative that embodies your brand's mission, seamlessly weaving in promotional elements.

Highlight Benefits, Not Features:

- Share how your product or service impacts lives rather than listing features.

Engage Through Emotion:

- Leverage emotional storytelling to forge connections between your audience and the essence of your narrative.

POTENTIAL PITFALLS AND HOW TO AVOID THEM

Knowing what to avoid can help you master your storytelling craft:

Over-Editing:

- While polishing is important, ensure you preserve the raw, human elements that make your story authentic and relatable.

Inconsistency:

- Maintain a consistent core narrative across all platforms to avoid confusing your audience and to strengthen your brand's identity.

Ignoring Feedback:

- Invite audience interaction and demonstrate openness to constructive feedback.

- Adapting your story based on their input shows you value their perspective and fosters deeper engagement.

Entrepreneurs who master these aspects of storytelling can turn potential challenges into opportunities for growth and connection.

By approaching storytelling with intentionality and care, you can create narratives that not only represent your brand authentically but also inspire and resonate with your audience in meaningful ways.

Once we understand the importance of maintaining authenticity and balance in your storytelling, it's clear that storytelling isn't just a business strategy—it's a journey of personal growth.

REFLECTIVE QUESTION:

What was the biggest challenge you faced when starting your side business?

How can you craft a story about overcoming that challenge, making it more actionable for the reader?

As you reflect on your challenge and how you overcame them, consider the broader impact of storytelling.

Beyond building your brand, it's a powerful tool for self-discovery and resilience.

By embracing the process of storytelling and engaging with your audience, you not only strengthen your brand but also embark on a path of self-discovery and resilience.

Let's explore how storytelling can be a powerful tool for personal development, enriching your life and the lives of those you connect with.

STORYTELLING AS PERSONAL GROWTH

Embracing storytelling is not only about crafting narratives for your brand; it's an enriching journey that fosters self-awareness and adaptability.

This personal growth process can be transformative, offering profound insights into who you are as an entrepreneur and a person.

THE POWER OF REFLECTION

Documenting and sharing your stories provides an opportunity to pause and reflect, helping you recognize the key moments and lessons that have defined your journey.

This practice encourages self-awareness by illuminating your strengths and areas for improvement, helping you adapt to new challenges with resilience.

Self-Awareness Through Reflection:

- By recounting past experiences, you gain clarity on what has shaped your journey.

- Whether it's celebrating successes or learning from failures, storytelling allows you to see the bigger picture and understand your evolution over time.

Adaptability Through Insight:

- Storytelling helps you adapt by encouraging a mindset that is open to learning and growth.

- By reflecting on past successes and failures, you gain a deeper understanding of your resilience and adaptability. These insights empower you to approach future uncertainties with confidence and creativity.

JOURNAL PROMPTS FOR REFLECTION

To deepen your journey of growth through storytelling, consider these journal prompts designed to reflect on your evolution as an entrepreneur:

1. Lessons from Failures:

- Reflect on a significant failure you've experienced.
- What emotions did you feel at the time?
- What lessons did you learn about your strengths and limitations?
- How has that experience shaped the way you approach challenges today?

2. Unexpected Successes:
   - Think of a time when success surprised you.
   - What small actions or decisions set this success in motion?
   - How did this experience expand your perspective on what's achievable?

3. Evolving Values:
   - Consider how your values have evolved throughout your entrepreneurial journey.
   - What pivotal experiences shaped this transformation?
   - How do these values guide your current business decisions and interactions?

4. Moments of Inspiration:
   - Reflect on a story—yours or someone else's—that deeply moved you.
   - What about the story resonated with you?
   - How did it shape your perspective or influence your actions?

5. Vision for the Future:
   - Visualize your future five years from now.

- What goals do you hope to achieve, personally and professionally?
- How do your present actions align with this vision, and which narratives will help you sustain momentum?

Engaging regularly with these prompts not only aids in personal reflection but also informs the stories you share with others.

As you grow, your narratives become richer, mirroring your journey of transformation and offering a compass for both personal and entrepreneurial endeavors.

Having delved into the ways storytelling promotes growth and adaptability, it's time to translate these insights into practical strategies for strengthening your brand and community connections.

By implementing key storytelling strategies, you can reinforce the narratives that not only define your brand but also inspire your community.

REFLECTION EXERCISE:

Reflect on a story where you demonstrated resilience in the face of adversity.

Consider what you learned from it and how this experience helped you define your path forward.

How can you share this with your audience that will engage and inspire them, encouraging them to draw strength and insight from your experience?

Let's synthesize these concepts into actionable steps that will enhance your storytelling journey and strengthen the connections you seek to build.

KEY TAKEAWAYS: TURNING INSIGHTS INTO ACTION

Effective storytelling has the power to elevate your brand while building authentic, lasting connections with your audience.

Let's solidify what you've learned and put it into action.

CRAFT YOUR STORY-DRIVEN POST - A STEP-BY-STEP GUIDE:

Step 1: Identify Your Core Message:

Clarify the main takeaway you want your audience to remember. Ground it in your brand's mission, vision, or values to ensure authenticity and alignment.

Step 2: Select a Compelling Anecdote:

Choose a real-life story that illustrates your core message.

Make it authentic and relatable, ensuring it resonates with your audience on a personal level.

Step 3: Define Your Audience:

Craft your story to align with the values, needs, and aspirations of your target audience.

Understanding their unique perspectives ensures your narrative strikes a chord.

Step 4: Draft the Narrative:

Develop a concise narrative that weaves in a relatable challenge, a pivotal turning point, and a compelling resolution.

Focus on authenticity to foster connection and trust.

Step 5: Include a Call-to-Action:

Motivate your audience to take action—share their own stories, explore your website, or connect with your brand in meaningful ways.

Step 6: Share on Social Media:

Leverage engaging visuals, compelling captions, and strategic timing to maximize visibility and encourage interaction on social media.

MASTER YOUR 3-MINUTE ELEVATOR PITCH

Step 1: Write Your Script:

Clearly define your brand's purpose, key values, and unique selling points.

Keep it concise, yet engaging.

Step 2: Perfect Your Delivery:

Practice aloud to ensure your message is both clear and compelling, refining your tone and pacing.

Step 3: Record with Purpose:

Prioritize clarity and enthusiasm while maintaining professionalism.

Use quality visuals and sound.

Step 4: Share Strategically:

Distribute your video on platforms where your audience is most active, and tailor your messaging to each channel.

Reflect and Adapt

- Evaluate the effectiveness of your storytelling by analyzing audience responses and engagement metrics.

- Stay adaptable, refining your approach based on constructive feedback and emerging trends.

Step 5: Celebrate Failures and Successes

- Embrace Vulnerability

- Share stories of setbacks and how you overcame them to humanize your brand and connect on a deeper level.

- Frame Success as Growth

- Celebrate milestones not as endpoints, but as chapters in your ongoing journey of learning and development.

DEVELOP A CONSISTENT STORYTELLING SCHEDULE

- Establish a content calendar to maintain a steady flow of storytelling.

- Strike a balance between promotional content and value-driven narratives to uphold authenticity and trust.

By implementing these steps, you not only tell stories that matter but also cultivate an environment where those stories can inspire and engage communities.

Remember, your stories are the heartbeat of your brand—make them resonate and enrich every interaction.

With these practical steps in your toolkit, you're poised to craft stories that not only speak to your brand's essence but also inspire and engage your community.

ACTION EXERCISE:

Draft a story about your new entrepreneurial journey that will engage your audience, inform them about your 'why,' define your brand, and inspire others.

Try it out on family or a close friend.

Note: Your story will likely go through many iterations over time. Don't expect it to be perfect.

As we conclude this chapter, let's reflect on how storytelling transforms your entrepreneurial journey into a tapestry of connections and shared values, setting the stage for continuous growth and discovery.

CONCLUSION AND SEGUE: CRAFTING YOUR LEGACY THROUGH STORIES

As we conclude this exploration, it's evident that storytelling transcends mere marketing—it's about crafting a legacy.

The stories you tell have the power to embed your brand into the lives of your audience, forging connections that last.

By weaving authenticity and emotion into your storytelling, you forge lasting connections that enhance your legacy. You cultivate a community that resonates with your brand's mission.

This not only strengthens customer ties, but also supports a resilient network that grows together through shared values and experiences. .

Storytelling is not just a tool for engagement; it's the foundation of enduring success and significance for your brand in a shifting landscape.

As we look ahead, aligning your brand's narrative with evolving market trends is crucial for staying true to both your business goals and personal values.

In Chapter 15, we'll explore strategies to integrate these components seamlessly, ensuring that your vision adapts effectively to the changing environment.

With storytelling as a powerful tool, you are equipped to embrace mentorship and achieve a balanced integration of your personal and professional life.

You will be prepared to strengthen your entrepreneurial journey, leading to lasting fulfillment and success.

CHAPTER 15

ALIGNING VISION WITH PROGRESS

INTRODUCTION: EMBRACING CHANGE, EMPOWERING VISION

Have you ever wondered whether holding firm to your vision is the key to your success or the challenge that's holding you back?

In the fast-paced world of entrepreneurship, aligning your vision with the ever-evolving market can be the difference between surviving and thriving.

This chapter explores how to stay true to your core mission while embracing change and progress.

Studies show that technology is essential for many small businesses.

About 85% of small businesses say technology helped them get started, and 94% report that it makes operations more efficient.

Furthermore, most businesses that use digital tools have seen increased customer growth and profitability.

Here's how companies have adapted to advancing technology:

Let's consider Peloton's journey.

Peloton initially aimed to revolutionize home fitness by offering live-streamed spinning classes, bringing the communal workout experience into the privacy of people's homes. Their stationary bikes and engaging virtual classes rapidly gained popularity.

Yet, with time, technology advanced and consumer preferences shifted, deeming a singular focus on spinning classes too narrow.

Peloton successfully expanded its offerings, introducing a wider range of fitness equipment, such as treadmills and rowing machines, while also diversifying into yoga, meditation, and strength training.

By integrating AI-driven features for real-time feedback, they elevated user experience on advanced digital platforms.

By aligning its core mission with technological trends, Peloton continued to thrive, highlighting the importance of a flexible vision in a dynamic market.

While Peloton's success illustrates how large corporations adapt, the same principles of vision alignment are crucial for small businesses as well.

Take Barbara's story, for example:

Barbara, a small business owner in her early 60s, owned and operated a local bookstore in her hometown for over 20 years. With the rise of e-books and online retailers, many small independent bookstores shuttered, but not Barbara's.

Instead of viewing digital technology as a threat, Barbara embraced it as an opportunity to grow her business.

Facing the unknowns of the digital world, Barbara took online courses tailored to small business owners.

She also hired a business coach specializing in online businesses, giving her the technical knowledge and confidence to begin her new journey.

Overwhelmed at first by the complexity of e-commerce platforms and digital marketing, Barbara confronted these challenges head-on, taking them one step at a time.

Soon, she was hosting virtual book clubs and author meet-and-greets, building a vibrant online community similar to the atmosphere at her physical store.

Before long, Barbara leveraged her years of experience by launching an online store, complementing her brick-and-mortar operations with curated reading lists and personalized recommendations.

This shift not only saved her business, but also demonstrated how integrating new tools with a steadfast vision can foster resilience and growth.

The stories of Peloton and Barbara illustrate key lessons in aligning vision with progress, reinforcing the idea that the heart of a successful business lies in its ability to adapt to a constantly changing world.

But what does it mean to have a dynamic vision, and how can you ensure your business goals align with both progress and your personal aspirations?

Let's explore how you can harness adaptability and vision alignment to build a sustainable legacy for your entrepreneurial journey.

Moving forward, we will explore the adaptability of your vision.

THE DYNAMIC NATURE OF VISION

In business, a 'vision' serves as both a lighthouse guiding you through uncharted waters and a flexible framework that responds to the ever-shifting tides of market dynamics.

A business vision is more than a statement; it's a flexible guide that shows your direction while allowing space for innovation.

Imagine your vision as a sturdy tree, rooted in core values and mission, yet flexible enough to sway with the winds of change.

This flexibility doesn't mean compromising on your business's core values; instead, it ensures your foundation remains strong while you grow and adapt in alignment with your true purpose.

Clarity in your vision is crucial.

Much like trying to navigate a journey without a map, a lack of clear vision can lead your business astray, hindering growth and misaligning efforts.

Clarity is achieved by embedding your core values into this vision, ensuring that every decision and action supports these fundamental principles.

Consider asking yourself:

What are the core values that drive my business?

How does my vision reflect these beliefs?

As you ponder these questions, remember that a truly dynamic vision is not just about pursuing growth; it's about ensuring that growth is meaningful and aligns with the principles you hold dear.

Consider, for example, Adam, the 62-year-old CPA with a lifelong passion for woodworking.

Adam's initial vision was to share his love of woodworking.

His journey began with opening an Etsy store to sell his handcrafted, high-quality pieces and share his woodworking with the world.

However, the market continued to evolve, and digital marketing became popular. As the market evolved, so did Adam's vision.

Understanding the importance of aligning with customer preferences, Adam leveraged his accounting expertise to refine his business strategies, and explored different marketing options.

With the rise of digital marketing, Adam vision adapted and he created a video course teaching woodworking skills online.

The constant evolution of Adam's vision exemplifies how adjusting one's vision—to market trends and technological trends and advancements—can expand a business's reach and influence.

Here are some guides on how to cultivate your business vision:

- Anchor Your Business in Core Values:

- Clearly define what matters most to your business, and let these values drive all your strategic decisions.

- Embrace Adaptability:

- Be open to adjusting your strategies in response to new opportunities or challenges, while remaining true to your mission.

- Maintain Clarity:

- Regularly revisit your vision to ensure it remains clear and aligned with your objectives.

Striking a balance between clarity and flexibility will help guide your business through challenges, ensuring you not only survive, but thrive.

With a clear and adaptable vision as the foundation, the next step is ensuring your business evolves alongside market shifts and remains aligned with your personal goals.

This will keep your business goals on track with your path to growth and opportunity.

Now that we've discussed the importance of clarity and adaptability, let's explore strategies to help you refine your vision.

As you do, you want to ensure that your business objectives remain aligned with your visions and goals of growth, opportunity, and your personal aspirations.

ACTION EXERCISE:

Write down at least three core values that you believe should guide your business decisions.

How do they align with your current goals?

Briefly outline your current business vision, highlighting parts that directly reflect your core values.

STRATEGIES FOR REFINING VISION

Refining your vision is a continuous journey that requires setting clear goals, adapting to market dynamics, and experimenting with new ideas.

Let's break these down into actionable strategies, starting with SMART goals.

SETTING SMART GOALS

SMART goals are a powerful tool for entrepreneurs, ensuring each objective is Specific, Measurable, Achievable, Relevant, and Time-bound.

Let's consider Jane, a fictional entrepreneur over 50, who owns a local bakery.

Implementing SMART Criteria, Jane might write her goals, as follows:

Specific:

- Clearly define what you want to achieve. Jane aims to boost her bakery's online sales.

Measurable:

- Use measurable metrics to track progress. For example, aiming for a 20% increase sets a clear, quantifiable target.

Achievable:

- Ensure the goal is realistic given your resources. Jane plans to leverage existing social media channels.

Relevant:

- Align the goal with broader business ambitions, like expanding reach through e-commerce.

Time-bound:

- Set a deadline. Jane gives herself six months to meet this target.

REASSESSING GOALS

After six months, Jane should review her results.

If her online sales surpass the 20% increase, she can set a more ambitious target.

If she falls short, she might evaluate her strategies and adjust her methods, perhaps by investing in new marketing tactics or seeking customer feedback.

ADAPTING TO MARKET DYNAMICS

Staying relevant requires staying attuned to current trends.

Engage these tools:

- Trend Analysis Software:

- Platforms like Google Trends can help you gauge consumer interest.

- Customer Feedback Surveys:

- Use online surveys to capture valuable insights about your customers' preferences and needs.

Engagement Steps:

1. Regularly review market reports.

2. Set up alerts for key industry keywords.

3. Establish a routine feedback system to adapt services based on the insights you gather.

PILOTING NEW INITIATIVES

Testing new ideas fosters innovation while minimizing risk. Here's a framework for piloting initiatives:

Define the Objective:

1. What change do you want to see?

2. For example, Jane might test a new pastry line.

Select a Test Group:

3. Select a segment of your audience for the initial rollout.

Collect Feedback:

4. Gather data on performance and customer response.

Analyze Results:

5. Evaluate the success based on set criteria.

Refine and Expand:

6. Adjust your approach before a broader launch, using feedback as a guide.

By setting SMART goals, adapting to market shifts, and thoughtfully piloting initiatives, you refine your business vision and ensure it thrives amidst evolving challenges.

ACTION EXERCISE:

Identify a specific area of your business you want to enhance, such as increasing sales.

Define your SMART goals to turn broad objectives into clear, actionable steps.

However, realizing your vision requires more than just strategic planning—it demands the alignment and empowerment of your leadership and team.

Next, we'll explore how fostering a supportive and innovative team culture can further propel your business , dynamic vision, and personal aspirations towards successful progress.

LEADERSHIP AND TEAM ALIGNMENT

Crafting a compelling vision and setting strategic goals are just the beginning.

The real impact comes when your leadership and team are fully aligned with these objectives, ready to innovate and adapt at every turn.

Design a leadership development program that fosters innovation, strategic thinking, and deep alignment with your business vision.

FOSTERING INNOVATIVE LEADERSHIP

CULTIVATING A CULTURE OF INNOVATION

Innovation thrives in environments where creativity is not only encouraged but celebrated.

As a leader, your role is to create a space where team members feel valued and inspired to bring their best ideas forward.

- Encourage Open Dialogue:

- Host regular brainstorming sessions and workshops where everyone can contribute ideas without fear of judgment.

- Recognize and Reward Creativity:

- Celebrate innovative ideas through recognition programs or small rewards to motivate your team continuously.

EMPOWERING TEAM MEMBERS

Empowerment stems from trust and the freedom to explore new possibilities.

By giving your team autonomy, you foster an environment where innovation becomes part of the organizational fabric.

- Delegate Authority:

- Empower team members to lead projects, fostering a sense of ownership and accountability.

- Provide Resources:

- Ensure your team has the tools and training necessary to further develop their ideas and skills further.

LEADERSHIP TRAINING AND MENTORSHIP

To maintain alignment and foster growth, focus on a leadership development program that blends strategic thinking with innovation.

CORE ELEMENTS OF A LEADERSHIP DEVELOPMENT PROGRAM

1. Strategic Thinking Workshops: Facilitate workshops to hone strategic planning skills, enabling

leaders to anticipate and address future challenges effectively.

2. Innovation Bootcamps:

3. Organize intensive sessions focused on creative problem-solving and innovation, incorporating real-world case studies to drive learning.

4. Mentorship Pairing:

5. Pair emerging leaders with experienced mentors who offer guidance, support, and fresh perspectives on navigating leadership challenges.

6. Feedback Loops:

7. Implement systems for regular feedback, enabling leaders to learn about their strengths and areas for improvement while fostering continuous development.

8. Vision Alignment Meetings:

9. Regularly revisit the core business vision with your leadership team to ensure strategic decisions align with long-term goals and values.

By designing a comprehensive leadership program that emphasizes strategic thinking and innovative practices, and fostering a culture that supports and nurtures these values, your business will be better equipped to adapt to and capitalize on emerging opportunities.

Next, we'll explore how personal growth can intersect with professional development, reinforcing a holistic approach to achieving your business vision.

INTEGRATING PERSONAL GROWTH

Embracing personal growth as part of your entrepreneurial journey enables a deeper alignment with your business vision.

Personal development isn't just beneficial for individual well-being; it's a catalyst for a thriving business.

Let's explore some practices and strategies to interweave your growth with your business ambitions.

SELF-REFLECTION AND JOURNALING

Regular reflection connects your evolving identity and aspirations with your business goals.

Here are three journaling prompts to guide your introspection:

1. "How have my personal insights or experiences this month influenced my business decisions?"
   - Reflect on recent personal insights and how they've shaped your strategic choices.
   - Identify shifts in perspective that may realign your business objectives with your core values.
2. "What strengths and growth areas have I identified, and how can they enhance my leadership?"
   - Acknowledge areas where you've excelled personally.

- Develop plans to leverage these strengths in your professional sphere, and outline steps to address any areas that need improvement.

3. "How can my personal passions enrich my business strategies and enhance our mission?"

- Explore how integrating your personal interests with business innovation could lead to unique opportunities.
- Create a plan to combine these passions with strategic objectives to foster creativity and enthusiasm within your team.

CONTINUOUS LEARNING

Lifelong learning drives both personal and professional growth, offering new insights and enhancing your capabilities.

- Online Courses and Webinars:

Enroll in courses that interest you and align with your business needs.

For example, learning digital marketing strategies can directly elevate your company's outreach efforts.

- Workshops and Conferences:

- Attend events to expand your industry knowledge and network, fostering both inspiration and collaboration.

BALANCING PERSONAL AND PROFESSIONAL GOALS

Balancing personal achievements with professional commitments is essential for sustainable success.

Set Boundaries:

Clearly define your work and personal time to maintain balance.

For instance, dedicate evenings to family or hobbies, reinforcing your personal well-being.

Personal Goal Setting:

Align personal goals, such as mastering a new skill or spending more time with loved ones, with your business objectives to create a more integrated approach.

Wellness Practices:

Incorporate activities like meditation or physical exercise to boost energy and resilience in both your personal and business life.

REFLECTIVE QUESTIONS:

1. How has a recent personal challenge or success informed my business approach or decision-making?

2. How could I incorporate my personal passions or hobbies into my business strategy to make it more fulfilling?

Connecting your personal growth journey with your business vision equips you to navigate the complexities of entrepreneurship with resilience and insight.

With this as your foundation, you have the opportunity to create a robust plan for enduring success that feeds into every aspect of your life.

Now, let's summarize these concepts into clear, actionable steps that will empower you to align your visionary path with ongoing progress, ensuring improved chances of success in the dynamic business landscape.

KEY TAKEAWAYS AND ACTION PLAN

Aligning your business vision with progress is essential for long-term success, helping you adapt, thrive, and capitalize on new opportunities.

Here's a practical action plan to help you achieve this alignment:

1. Craft a Dynamic Vision:

   - Define your vision as a flexible guide rooted in your core values.

   - Regularly revisit and refine your vision to ensure clarity and alignment with both personal and business goals.

2. Set SMART Goals:

   - Set goals using the SMART framework—Specific, Measurable, Achievable, Relevant, Time-bound.

   - Schedule periodic reviews to reassess and adjust goals as needed.

3. Adapt to Market Dynamics:

- Use tools like trend analysis software and customer feedback to stay informed about market changes.

- Engage actively with customer insights and adjust strategies accordingly.

4. Pilot New Initiatives:

- Test new ideas using a clear framework: define objectives, select test groups, gather feedback, and refine based on results.

- Scale successful initiatives thoughtfully.

5. Foster Leadership and Team Alignment:

- Create a leadership program that emphasizes strategic thinking and innovation.

- Foster a culture in which team members feel empowered and invested in the company's vision.

6. Integrate Personal Growth:

- Engage in self-reflection to align personal insights with business strategy.

- Balance your personal and professional goals to achieve holistic success.

Aligning your business vision with ongoing progress is not a static journey; it is a dynamic process.

By employing these strategies with commitment and flexibility, you're well-equipped to flourish and adapt amidst change and challenge.

You now possess the skills to turn challenges into stepping stones for growth and success.

As we conclude this chapter, let's look ahead to explore how these strategies empower your journey toward personal fulfillment and professional achievement.

CONCLUSION: THRIVING THROUGH ALIGNMENT AND PROGRESS

Flexibility, vision alignment, and empowered leadership are the cornerstones of sustained success in business.

Embracing adaptability allows you to not only react to changes, but also proactively shape your path to seize new opportunities.

This chapter underscores how aligning your business vision with ongoing progress creates a strong foundation, ensuring your enterprise not only survives, but thrives amidst the uncertainties of today's ever-changing market landscape.

As explored in Chapter 15, the key to thriving in a fast-paced world lies in how well you align your visionary path with ongoing progress.

Whether by setting insightful SMART goals, piloting new initiatives, or weaving personal growth into your professional life, each strategy contributes to a tapestry of resilience and innovation.

Remember, successful alignment of your visionary path fosters a journey where businesses not only withstand the tests of time, but also evolve dynamically, continually capturing new opportunities.

As you build upon these insights and we celebrate the transformative journey you're embarking on, you are well-equipped with the wisdom and inspiration to turn your passions into profits and navigate whatever the future holds.

Based on what we've learned, it's clear that nurturing these newfound insights is crucial.

Mentorship can guide us, but true empowerment comes from balancing personal joy with professional triumphs.

Now, let's now explore strategies that enhance your growth and harmonize your life in Chapter 16: Empowerment for a Brighter Future.

CHAPTER 16

EMPOWERMENT FOR A BRIGHTER FUTURE

CHARTING NEW PATHS: MY JOURNEY

Throughout my career as a physician specializing in Geriatric and Adult Psychiatry, I found deep fulfillment in helping improve the lives of my patients. But when life called me to step back from my practice to care for my aging father, I found myself at a crossroads.

For me, retirement wasn't an end—it was a launchpad for new beginnings. My lifelong calling to help others remained just as strong. The question was: How?

I exchanged my therapist's couch for the fast-paced world of entrepreneurship, driven by a mission to empower others. The transition, however, was far from smooth. Stepping into the unfamiliar realm of online marketing and entrepreneurship was daunting.

But my deep-seated desire to help others achieve personal and financial well-being propelled me forward. I saw the potential of digital and network marketing to help individuals build side hustles from the ground up. Harnessing the power of AI, I founded Mastering Your Wellbeing Inc.—

not just as a business, but as a movement to promote financial freedom and a better life for many.

My journey is proof that embracing change and applying existing skills in new ways can open doors to a brighter future. I overcame the fear of leaving a familiar field and used my knowledge as a healer to create something innovative and impactful.

So, how can you leverage your unique skills and experiences to forge your own path?

Like many professionals over 50, I faced the challenge of stepping into an entirely new industry. But I discovered that entrepreneurship isn't just about business—it's about vision, connection, and creating a legacy of empowerment.

By welcoming change and leveraging the tools of our time, we can redefine success and inspire lasting transformation in our lives and the lives of others.

Now, let's explore how a clear, adaptable vision can propel you toward a brighter future.

Many of the themes we've explored throughout this book come together in this chapter. Here, we'll dive into how knowledge, technology, and community can drive systematic change—fostering not only financial independence but also personal and professional fulfillment.

EMPOWERMENT THROUGH PERSONAL GROWTH

Rediscovering your passions can be a transformative experience, especially when paired with the invaluable skills honed over decades of professional growth.

According to research from Legal Zoom, 31% of new business owners cite passion as their primary motivator, while over 60% launch ventures out of dissatisfaction with corporate America.

For many, transformation begins by looking beyond their current roles and reigniting their passions.

The key lies in blending years of professional expertise with personal interests to create a business that inspires others.

Here are three ways with accompanying exercises that professionals can use to unearth and repurpose these skills to embark on exciting new business ventures:

1. REFLECT AND RECOGNIZE YOUR SKILLS

The journey toward empowerment begins with honest reflection.

Look back at your career—what skills have you developed?

Whether it's leadership, project management, or problem-solving, these abilities are not confined to one job or industry.

I, for example, drew on his deep understanding of human behavior from psychiatry to develop keen insights into market needs and consumer needs.

By repurposing his expertise, he successfully bridged the gap between two seemingly unrelated fields.

Exercise:

- Take 10 minutes to list skills you frequently used in your previous roles.

- Next to each, note how they could be applied in a new context.

2. ENGAGE IN PASSION PROJECTS

We often find our deepest passions in the projects that energize and excite us the most.

Think about the hobbies or side projects you've enjoyed outside of work.

Are there skills within these activities that could translate into a new business?

This form of engagement not only enriches your personal life but also often plants the seeds for professional possibilities.

Exercise:

- Reflect on a hobby you love.

- Write down three skills involved in this hobby that can be applicable to a business setting.

3. NETWORK AND COLLABORATE FOR NEW PERSPECTIVES

Leveraging existing networks can open new opportunities and provide fresh perspectives on how skills can serve new markets.

Networking doesn't just open doors to new opportunities; it also provides insights into how different industries function and where transferable skills may apply.

For instance, drawing from experience with medical networks helped create a strong foundation for a business that aligned with the values of the health and wellness community.

Joining a coaching program, connecting with groups of new entrepreneurs, and finding an accountability partner for one-on-one coaching and collaboration were instrumental in fostering growth.

Exercise: Identify three people in your professional circle who have successfully transitioned into new fields. Reach out to them for advice and inspiration.

REFLECTION EXERCISE:

What are three passions or hobbies you've always dreamed of exploring?

How might they translate into a viable business idea?

What skills from your previous career could you repurpose to help create and build this new business?

Transitioning skills into entrepreneurship is a shared endeavor—one that thrives on community and collaboration. By fostering a community around shared passions and expertise, a wealth of experience can turn into an innovative new venture.

Equipped with a renewed sense of purpose and a robust network, the next step in the entrepreneurial journey involves embracing the tools of our modern age. By harnessing technology, both personal growth and systemic change can be driven, paving the way to a future where innovation guides success.

Now, let's explore how embracing technology can open doors to transformation, fulfillment, and entrepreneurial success.

HARNESSING TECHNOLOGY FOR INNOVATION

In today's digital landscape, technology is more than a tool—it's a driving force for innovation and transformation in business.

For many professionals over 50, adopting new technology can feel overwhelming at first. However, learning has no age limits and offers substantial personal and professional benefits.

With the right mindset, learning in small steps can lead to significant achievements. By embracing technology with confidence and persistence, it can become a powerful partner in the entrepreneurial journey.

EMBRACING TECHNOLOGY WITH CONFIDENCE AND PURPOSE

Imagine the transformative potential of tools like AI, enabling businesses to streamline operations, enhance efficiency, and connect with broader audiences.

Digital marketing platforms can propel messages to global audiences, while AI tools can automate customer service, freeing up time to focus on innovation.

Every step into technology is a step towards efficiency and growth.

PRACTICAL STRATEGY 1: START WITH SMALL STEPS

Begin by identifying one key area of business that could benefit from automation or digital tools.

For example, implementing an email marketing campaign or scheduling social media posts using online platforms can create immediate efficiencies.

PRACTICAL STRATEGY 2: LEARN THROUGH BEGINNER-FRIENDLY COURSES

Take advantage of beginner-friendly online courses on platforms like Coursera and Udemy. These courses offer accessible introductions to topics like AI, digital marketing, and automation.

OVERCOMING COMMON FEARS

Many people wonder, "How can I adapt to this new wave of technology?" Like others, initial hesitation and doubts about navigating unfamiliar technology are natural.

However, through curiosity and a willingness to learn, apprehension can be transformed into confidence. Over time, sharing learned insights with others helps reinforce this growth and fosters a community of learners.

When venturing into AI to build Mastering Your Wellbeing Inc., simple AI applications were introduced to streamline customer interactions and enhance data management.

This journey has shown that mastery isn't required all at once—progress is made one tool, one lesson at a time.

MY JOURNEY INTO TECHNOLOGY AND ENTREPRENEUR-SHIP

My leap into the entrepreneurial tech world began with small, manageable steps, each building my confidence along the way.

By integrating AI-powered tools into my business, I was able to personalize customer interactions, significantly boosting engagement and satisfaction.

This transformation didn't just revitalize my business model—it reshaped my entire approach to entrepreneurship, making it more agile and responsive to customer needs.

Facing challenges in entrepreneurship is inevitable. With the right strategies, these obstacles can become opportunities for growth.

PRACTICAL SOLUTIONS FOR OVERCOMING CHALLENGES

Solution 1:

Seek out a mentor or a tech-savvy peer who can guide you through the initial stages of your learning journey.

Guidance from those comfortable with technology can make the transition easier and more approachable.

Solution 2:

Join online forums or communities dedicated to your chosen technology.

These platforms provide a space to ask questions, share experiences, and collaborate with others on similar journeys.

Success isn't limited to those with a tech background; rather, it belongs to those willing to embrace continuous learning. How might technology shape the way you redefine success in your business?

As I adopt new technological innovations, I consider how these tools can strengthen connections, amplifying both business success and personal growth.

Technology is not just a catalyst for efficiency and growth—it's a powerful bridge for building and nurturing meaningful networks.

Online platforms and digital tools offer vast opportunities to connect with others who share similar goals and passions, enabling collaborative ventures that transcend geographical barriers.

By leveraging technology to expand my network, I'm not merely adopting new tools—I'm fostering a dynamic community where shared knowledge and support fuel success.

As we move into discussing the importance of community, think about how your online connections can enhance your personal growth and broaden the impact you have within your audience.

REFLECTIVE QUESTION:

What technology skill feels most intimidating to you, and why?

How could overcoming this fear unlock new growth opportunities for your business?

BUILDING AND NURTURING COMMUNITY

In the world of entrepreneurship, success is not a solo act.

Instead, it's a shared journey that thrives on the strength of community.

By building a robust network, you not only create a support system but also open doors to new ideas, opportunities, and collective growth.

Communities can offer a wealth of knowledge and a sense of belonging that propels you toward your goals.

THE ROLE OF NETWORKS IN ENTREPRENEURSHIP

Entrepreneurial networks act as incubators for innovation and resilience.

They provide a platform where like-minded individuals can exchange ideas, share resources, and offer support.

Take Mary Smith as an example: At 55, she transitioned from a long corporate career to launching a consulting business specializing in sustainable practices.

She used her extensive professional network to ease this transition.

By reaching out to former colleagues, joining online forums, and attending industry events, she found like-minded people eager to help.

Her network not only provided valuable advice, but also introduced her to her first clients. Her success story shows how valuable connections can be when starting something new later in life.

One of the groups Mary joined was the TED Community.

The TED Community exemplifies a thriving network where entrepreneurial innovation flourishes.

Known for its ability to inspire and connect leaders from diverse fields, TED fosters a culture where innovation is born from shared knowledge and collaboration.

Local events like TEDx, inspire individuals to engage with big transformative ideas and connect with others passionate about driving change.

BUILDING YOUR OWN COMMUNITY

Creating your own entrepreneurial network might seem like a daunting task, but with clear steps and intentionality, you can construct a community that uplifts and sustains:

- Start with Shared Values:

- Define the core principles that guide your business.

- Seek others who align with these ideas to form meaningful connections.

- Attend Relevant Events:

- Explore both virtual and in-person events tailored to your industry.

- These settings provide opportunities to meet potential collaborators and mentors.

- Leverage Social Media:

- Use platforms like LinkedIn or niche industry groups to connect with others, share insights, and build a professional presence.

- Participate actively in discussions and share your expertise to establish credibility and foster meaningful connections.

- Create a Mastermind Group:

- Form or join a mastermind group—a collective of entrepreneurs who meet regularly to exchange ideas, tackle challenges, and provide mutual accountability.

- This not only aids personal growth but creates a strong bond through shared experiences.

- Offer Value First:

- Approach networking with a mindset of giving.

- Offering support and sharing valuable insights cultivates a cycle of reciprocity, which strengthens and enriches your network.

As you build connections and offer value, your network transforms into a thriving ecosystem where collaboration fosters innovation and mutual success.

SUCCESS THROUGH COLLABORATION

When you nurture and invest in your network, it doesn't just grow—it thrives.

Consider how the TED Community continually births collaborative successes by offering members a space to share and learn.

Your network can function in much the same way, becoming a hive of innovation and support as you navigate the entrepreneurial landscape.

How might strengthening your network redefine your journey towards success?

With a strong community to nurture your journey, the next step is to consider how you define success on your own terms.

By aligning your personal values with your professional aspirations, you can create a path that not only meets traditional markers of achievement but also fulfills you deeply.

Let's explore how this personal alignment can transform your entrepreneurial pursuits into a legacy of empowerment and innovation.

DEFINING AND REDEFINING SUCCESS

For entrepreneurs over 50, redefining success offers an opportunity to align professional goals with personal values and aspirations.

As priorities evolve, this stage of life provides a chance to merge professional goals with personal meaning, creating a more rewarding entrepreneurial path.

ALIGNING VALUES WITH GOALS

True success transcends financial metrics, focusing instead on the fulfillment derived from pursuing what genuinely matters.

By integrating personal values like community, creativity, or sustainability into your business goals, you can create ventures that not only prosper but also enrich your life and the lives of others.

Example: Inclusive Entrepreneurship

Arlan Hamilton offers an inspiring example of redefining success by challenging conventional norms in the venture capital industry.

As the founder of Backstage Capital, Hamilton focused on inclusive entrepreneurship, creating opportunities for underrepresented minorities in tech.

Her story illustrates how aligning with values such as diversity and inclusion can drive both business success and meaningful societal change.

REFLECTIVE QUESTIONS

To help you articulate your unique definition of success, consider these questions:

- What are the core values I want my business to embody?

- How can my work align with these values and contribute to my overall life satisfaction?

- How do I define success beyond financial achievements?

Embracing a values-driven approach to success doesn't just redefine your career—it sets the foundation for a meaningful legacy.

Pursuing goals aligned with your core beliefs offers a unique opportunity to translate those intentions into leadership that inspires and uplifts.

In the following section, we'll examine how purposeful leadership can help you build a legacy that magnifies your impact and drives systemic change.

LEGACY BUILDING THROUGH LEADERSHIP

Building a legacy through leadership goes beyond personal achievements; it centers on the lasting impact you create in the lives of others.

Mentorship emerges as a powerful conduit for legacy building, allowing leaders to extend their impact far beyond personal reach.

MENTORSHIP: A CORNERSTONE OF LEGACY BUILDING

Through mentorship, you impart knowledge, skills, and values to others, fostering a cycle of continuous growth and empowerment.

As mentors guide and nurture future leaders, they create ripples of influence that can transform industries and communities.

This approach ensures that a leader's legacy not only endures, but also grows, amplified by the achievements of those they've inspired.

CASE STUDY: OPRAH WINFREY

Oprah Winfrey exemplifies how mentorship and education can shape a lasting legacy, influencing countless lives across generations.

Beyond her media accomplishments, Oprah has invested significantly in mentoring efforts, most notably through the Oprah Winfrey Leadership Academy for Girls in South Africa.

This initiative showcases how investing in education and personal development can uplift generations, cultivating leaders who carry forward the vision of empowerment and change.

ACTIONABLE STEPS TO CULTIVATE LEADERSHIP

For entrepreneurs over 50 aiming to leave a lasting legacy, here are practical steps to foster leadership within your teams or communities:

- Establish Mentorship Programs:

- Create platforms where emerging leaders can learn from experienced mentors.

- Sharing your experiences helps perpetuate knowledge and wisdom, empowering others to achieve their full potential.

- Encourage Open Dialogue:

- Cultivate an environment where ideas and questions are encouraged.

- Open communication fosters trust and accelerates personal and professional growth.

- Recognize and Develop Potential:

- Look for leadership qualities within your team.

- Support training and development initiatives that help individuals realize their potential.

- Lead by Example:

- Demonstrate the behaviors and values you wish to see in others.

- Authentic leadership inspires respect and emulation.

As you engage in mentorship, think about how you want your influence to be perceived in the years to come.

When you empower others, you create not only a lasting legacy, but also a brighter future that reflects your values and vision.

With the principles of leadership and legacy building established, it's time to translate your vision into actionable steps.

By crafting a clear and focused plan, you can strategically align your unique skills, values, and goals to drive meaningful change.

Let's explore how to create a detailed vision and action plan that not only guides your business but also propels you toward a future rich with possibilities and fulfillment.

PRACTICAL EXERCISE: CRAFT YOUR VISION AND ACTION PLAN

Creating a clear and compelling vision is pivotal to guiding your entrepreneurial journey, serving as your North Star that informs every decision you make.

Setting actionable goals alongside this vision ensures your path is both aspirational and practical, paving the way for achievable success.

CRAFTING A CLEAR AND INSPIRING VISION STATEMENT

Your vision statement should encapsulate the essence of what you aspire to achieve through your business.

It should reflect your core values and serve as a motivational beacon.

Identify and Reflect on Your Passions:

Think about what motivates and excites you.

What meaningful changes do you envision for your industry or community?

Visualize and Define Your Future:

Envision your business in the next five to ten years. Who are you serving, and what impact are you making?

Draft a Compelling Vision Statement:

Combine these elements into a concise, powerful statement.

Aim for clarity and inspiration to encapsulate your business's future.

SETTING ACTIONABLE GOALS

Once your vision is clear, the next step is to establish actionable goals that transform your aspirations into tangible results.

Here's a step-by-step guide:

Identify Key Milestones:

Break your vision into smaller, achievable goals that act as stepping stones.

Set SMART Goals:

Ensure each goal is Specific, Measurable, Achievable, Relevant, and Time-bound.

Design a Step-by-Step Action Plan:

For each goal, list the necessary steps to achieve it within a set timeline.

Monitor and Adjust:

Regularly review and adjust your progress to stay aligned with your vision.

EXAMPLE: MY VISION-DRIVEN DECISIONS

I harnessed my vision of promoting well-being through innovative side hustles to shape my business strategies.

By focusing on digital and network marketing with an emphasis on AI tools, I ensured that every decision aligned with my goal of empowering others.

This clear vision enabled me to make strategic choices that kept my business on a path of growth and impact.

EXERCISE WORKSHEET:

See The Passion Project Playbook Business Roadmap Worksheet.

Reflect on these steps and fill out the exercise worksheet to position your business for success.

- Vision Statement: Write a draft of your vision statement based on your reflections.

- Milestones: Identify at least three key milestones for the next year.

- SMART Goals: Create one SMART goal for each milestone with actionable steps.

- Review Schedule: Decide how often you will review your progress and adjust your plan.

By articulating my vision and setting immediate, realistic goals, I take proactive steps toward my business future.

As I actively engage with my vision and set purposeful goals, I recognize the importance of celebrating each milestone along the way. Acknowledging progress not only reinforces achievements but also nurtures the drive for continual growth and transformation.

Now, let's explore how celebrating successes can reinforce my journey of empowerment and fulfillment.

CELEBRATING PROGRESS AND IMPACT

In the entrepreneurial journey, celebrating milestones is vital for sustaining momentum and cultivating a sense of accomplishment.

Acknowledging these moments fuels my passion and strengthens the collective spirit of my community, emphasizing that every small step is a meaningful victory toward greater achievements.

THE TRANSFORMATIVE POWER OF RECOGNIZING ACHIEVEMENTS

Acknowledgment fosters empowerment by affirming that efforts are producing meaningful results.

Each milestone, no matter how small, signifies progress and provides motivation to keep moving forward.

By honoring these achievements, I build a positive, resilient mindset that celebrates growth and accomplishment.

IDEAS FOR CELEBRATING MILESTONES

Involving my community in these celebrations amplifies the impact of achievements and strengthens connections.

Here are some ways to engage others in celebrating progress:

- Host a Virtual Event: Organize a virtual gathering to unite my team and community, sharing success stories and key lessons to inspire collective growth.

- Share Stories: Use social media platforms to highlight milestones and express gratitude to those who supported me.

- Create a Wall of Wins: Design a 'Wall of Wins,' either physical or virtual, to showcase achievements and display inspiring quotes from those who contributed to my success.

- Community Givebacks: Mark significant milestones with community service or charitable contributions to reflect the values of my mission.

HARNESSING THE POWER OF SMALL WINS

Celebrating milestones sustains momentum and inspires greater achievements throughout your entrepreneurial journey.

Each small win contributes to the overall success of your journey, acting as stepping stones towards your vision.

These victories instill confidence and reaffirm your strategic direction, making every step an integral part of the larger narrative.

By creating a culture of celebration, you not only motivate yourself but also influence those around you to aspire towards their goals.

Each milestone you celebrate along your entrepreneurial journey weaves together the threads of knowledge, technology, and community, forming a vibrant tapestry of empowerment and growth.

This chapter's insights remind us that true success is a journey of continuous growth and impact.

Let's reflect on how embracing this path can lead to profound personal and collective change.

EMPOWERMENT UNLEASHED: A JOURNEY OF TRANSFORMATION

As I reflect on this chapter and approach the end of this book, I am reminded that empowerment through entrepreneurship is not just a goal but an evolving journey filled with new possibilities.

This journey encourages me to go beyond conventional limits and carve a path that aligns with both my personal and professional aspirations.

Throughout this chapter, I have explored how combining knowledge, technology, and community can drive financial independence and fulfillment.

From my own transition from medicine to online marketing entrepreneurship to the power of shared networks and clear vision statements, each experience and strategy has reinforced that entrepreneurship is a continuous learning process and an opportunity to build something meaningful.

Empowerment is not a destination but an ongoing voyage—one that offers both personal satisfaction and collective support.

By embracing my unique journey, I not only create change in my own life but also contribute to a broader movement of innovation and growth.

So, what will my next step be? What kind of impact can I create through my entrepreneurial endeavors?

The journey is mine to shape, full of opportunities to redefine success in a way that is authentic to me and those I aim to serve.

I will take this moment to move forward with confidence and purpose, turning aspirations into reality and shaping a future that benefits both myself and others.

ACTION EXERCISE:

To take the first step, I will share my goals with a peer or an accountability partner.

Together, we can support and motivate each other to turn our dreams and passions into reality.

CHAPTER 17

THE EPILOGUE

As we conclude this journey, let's reflect on the core themes that have shaped our path:

- the transformative power of passion,

- the resilience of innovation,

- and the courage to embrace fresh beginnings at any stage of life.

Each chapter has explored the potential of aligning personal passions and dreams with professional endeavors, revealing the profound impact this harmony can have on your life and the world at large.

Use these lessons as your blueprint for success.

By channeling your unique passions, embracing digital tools, and cultivating supportive networks, you are empowered to redefine success on your own terms.

Remember, entrepreneurship extends beyond launching a business—it's about building a legacy, creating a meaningful impact, and finding lasting fulfillment.

As we've touched on before, businesses that combine their passion with their prior experiences tend to have a higher success rate.

A Legal Zoom study, citing the National Bureau of Economic Research, found that businesses aligned with an entrepreneur's prior experience often grow significantly faster.

In some cases, they're up to 125% more likely to achieve high growth.

According to Score.org:

- Over half (54%) of America's small business owners are aged 50 or older.

- Among these owners, 67% report their businesses are profitable.

- Additionally, 76% rate their happiness at 8 or higher on a 10-point scale.

So now is the time for action.

Your insights and reflections can help serve as catalysts for transformation.

They urge you to take that first, bold step toward building a business that resonates with your passion.

Identify those initial steps, lean into the excitement of new beginnings, and wield your vision as a beacon guiding you forward.

Allow me to introduce Ginny, a retired family counselor with a passion for fostering better communication within families.

Her story exemplifies the transformative power of passion, innovation, and action.

Ginny's dream was to write a book to share her knowledge and help intergenerational families work together to find common ground through healthy communication.

Ginny, a vibrant mature woman, once stood at the crossroads of curiosity and fear when it came to AI.

Initially, Ginny felt apprehensive about Artificial Intelligence, perceiving it as an unfamiliar and insurmountable challenge.

Although she'd heard how many people had adopted ChatGPT, and were doing amazing things with it, she felt it was a tool that was beyond her grasp.

However, encouraged by her daughter, she decided to take a leap of faith.

She reached out for coaching and embarked on a transformative journey.

Over the course of a few weeks, Ginny's story unfolded in ways she never imagined.

Under guidance and coaching, she signed up for ChatGPT.

With just a few instructions and virtual guidance through Zoom, Ginny quickly discovered that using AI tools was far simpler than she had anticipated.

In fact, she was able to quickly draft an outline for her book, a task she believed would take years to manage on her own.

Within weeks, she had not only completed the first draft but was also creating books for her beloved grandchildren.

In a heartfelt moment during one of our calls, Ginny offered a spontaneous testimonial that encapsulated her journey:

"Without your guidance, I never envisioned completing my book. What I thought would take years became a reality in weeks. You brought my dream to life."

Ginny's transformation is a testament to the power of guidance, perseverance, and the courage to embrace new technologies.

Stories like Ginny's remind us that transformation begins with the decision to embrace change and take the first step toward our goals.

Her journey from a hesitant observer of AI to an author on track to publishing her book serves as an inspiration for us all, proving that with the right support and tools, dreams can become reality.

As you stand at the threshold of endless possibilities, let the excitement of new opportunities propel you forward.

This is your moment to transform aspirations into achievements and turn dreams into reality.

The possibilities are endless, and with every step you take, the path becomes clearer.

What first step will you take right now?

What will your legacy be, and how will you begin shaping it today?

Move forward with optimism, equipped with knowledge and driven by passion.

The world awaits what only you can offer if you choose to start your journey and explore the wealth of opportunities that are in front of you.

Step into this journey with confidence, trusting in your ability to achieve remarkable success and fulfillment by turning your passions into profits.

Your next step is entirely yours to take—only you can set it in motion.

If you're inspired to begin your journey in launching a thriving online digital marketing business, now is the moment to take action.

Approach the journey ahead with courage and determination.

The world is ready to be transformed by your unique talents, vision, and passion.

With warm wishes for your success, happiness, and fulfillment!

- Doug

ABOUT THE AUTHOR

Doug Kalunian is a retired psychiatrist turned online entrepreneur and business coach with more than 30 years of experience improving the lives of others through care, education, and mentorship. Inspired by his own journey of leaving a full-time career to care for his aging father, Doug developed a passion for guiding others to create online businesses aligned with their passions, skills, and goals.

As the founder of Mastering Your Wellbeing Inc, Doug specializes in empowering individuals aged 45 and older to transform their financial futures and personal lives by building sustainable side hustle businesses using the power of AI. His expertise combines a deep understanding of personal growth with practical strategies for navigating the challenges of online entrepreneurship.

THE PASSION PROJECT PLAYBOOK
BUSINESS ROADMAP WORKSHEET

INSTRUCTIONS

1. VISION STATEMENT

The ultimate goal of a vision statement is to outline three key goals, to help guide the business toward achieving success.

Effective vision statements generally include:

- What you want your organization to accomplish; what is the purpose of the business

- Who you want to serve - Your ideal target audience

- The outcomes you want the business to achieve.

Instructions:

- Write a short sentence or two that address the three key elements, above.

- Focus on what you'd like to achieve, for whom, and how your business will help them.

- Keep it clear, simple, and easy to remember

Example: "My dream is to build an online store that offers budget-friendly cooking classes, helping people everywhere eat healthy meals at home."

2. MILESTONES

Instructions:

1. Think of 2–3 big achievements you want by the end of the year.

2. Make them aspirational, but achievable

3. Don't focus solely on financial achievements.

Examples of Milestones:

- Finish designing and launching your website.

- Sign up your first 10 paying customers.

- Create a blog or video series to share your expertise.

3. SMART GOALS

Instructions:

- For each milestone, set one SMART goal:

  o Specific: Clearly state what you want to accomplish.

  o Measurable: Show how you'll measure success (numbers, deadlines, etc.).

  o Achievable: Choose a goal that's within reach with your skills and resources.

- ○ Relevant: Make sure it connects to your vision and milestones.

- ○ Time-Bound: Set a firm deadline.

Example for Milestone 1 (Website Launch):

- SMART Goal:

- "I will finish my website by April 30, including all main pages and a simple checkout system."

  - ○ Action Steps:

    1. Pick a website platform and theme by March 1.

    2. Write the content for each page by March 15.

    3. Set up payment options by April 15.

    4. Test everything and fix issues by April 25.

4. REVIEW SCHEDULE

Instructions:

- Decide how often you'll check on your progress.

  - ○ This could be weekly, monthly, or at certain key points (like after a product launch).

- Use these reviews to note what's working, what isn't, and what to do next.

Example:

"I'll review my goals on the first Monday of every month to measure sales, new leads, and website traffic. If needed, I'll adjust any milestone to keep things on track."

THE PASSION PROJECT PLAYBOOK BUSINESS ROADMAP WORKSHEET

WORKSHEET

1. My Vision Statement:

   ○ _____
     _____

   ○ _____
     _____

2. My Milestones (for next year):

   ○ Milestone 1:
     _____

   ○ Milestone 2:
     _____

   ○ Milestone 3:
     _____

3. My SMART Goals & Action Steps:

   ○ For Milestone 1:

   ▪ SMART Goal:

   _____

   ▪ Action Steps:

   1. _____

   2. _____

   3. _____

   ○ For Milestone 2:

   ▪ SMART Goal:

   _____

   ▪ Action Steps:

   1. _____

   2. _____

   3. _____

   ○ For Milestone 3:

   ▪ SMART Goal:

   _____

   ▪ Action Steps:

   1. _____

2. _____

3. _____

4. My Review Schedule:

   ○ How often will I review my goals?

_____

_____

Use this worksheet to map out your business vision, milestones, and goals. Keep it somewhere you can see it often. By reviewing your progress, you'll stay on track and keep moving forward.

COMPREHENSIVE GLOSSARY OF KEY BUSINESS AND LEGAL TERMS

A

- **A/B Testing:** A method of comparing two versions of a webpage, email, or other marketing asset to identify which performs better. By altering a single variable, such as a headline or button color, marketers gather data to optimize performance based on user responses.

- **Affiliate Marketing:** A type of performance-based marketing where a business rewards affiliates for each visitor or customer brought by the affiliate's own marketing efforts.

- **Artificial Intelligence (AI):** The simulation of human intelligence processes by machines, especially computer systems, including learning, reasoning, and self-correction.

- **Asset:** Any resource owned by an individual or entity that is expected to provide future economic benefits. Assets can include physical items like machinery and buildings, as well as intangible items like patents and trademarks.

- Articles of Incorporation: Documents filed with a governmental body to legally establish the creation of a corporation. These documents typically include the corporation's name, purpose, authorized number of shares, classes of stock, and other conditions.

B

- Brand: A set of marketing and communication methods that help to distinguish a company from competitors and create a lasting impression in the minds of customers.

- Blockchain: A decentralized database that maintains a growing list of records, verified across a network of computers, and secured with timestamps and transaction data. Blockchain acts as a secure digital ledger, permanently recording transactions in a way that is nearly impossible to alter.

- Business Plan: A formal document outlining a business's goals, strategies for achieving them, and the timeline for implementation.

C

- C Corporation (C-Corp): A legal structure for a corporation in which the owners or shareholders are taxed separately from the entity. Corporations are subject to corporate taxes, and income taxes on dividends paid to shareholders.

- Capital: Financial assets needed for a business to produce the goods or services it sells. This includes physical goods such as equipment used in production and financial assets.

- Cash Flow: The total amount of money being transferred into and out of a business, especially as it affects liquidity.

- Copyright: A form of protection granted by law for original works of authorship. It covers both published and unpublished works, including literary, and certain other intellectual works.

- Corporation: A legal entity that is separate and distinct from its owners, providing limited liability protections but subject to corporate tax rates.

- Customer Acquisition Cost (CAC): The total cost associated with acquiring a new customer, including marketing and sales expenses.

- Customer Journey Mapping: The process of visually mapping a customer's interactions with a brand across various touchpoints. This tool helps businesses understand the customer experience, identify pain points, and optimize interactions to enhance customer satisfaction and engagement.

D

- Digital Marketing: The component of marketing that utilizes internet and online-based digital technologies such as desktop computers, mobile phones, and other digital media platforms to promote products and services.

- Disclaimer: A statement disclaiming responsibility, designed to limit civil liability for specific acts or omissions.

- Disclosures: Statements that provide important information to consumers about a product or service, often required by law to ensure transparency and consumer protection.

- Doing Business As (DBA): Some businesses are run under a different name than what is legally registered. This is where a DBA is used. There are often different requirements for filing a DBA based on your state, county or city. It's important to investigate the requirements for your situation.

E

- E-commerce: The act of buying or selling products and services over electronic systems such as the internet.

- Employer Identification Number (EIN): A nine-digit number assigned by the Internal Revenue Service (IRS) to identify business in the United States for tax purposes. Also known as a Federal Tax Identification Number.

- Equity: Ownership in an asset such as a company, represented by shares that are issued to investors.

F

- Fiscal Year: A one-year period used by governments and businesses for accounting and budget purposes.

- Franchise: A business model in which a company licenses its brand and operations to another party in exchange for fees or royalties.

I

- Intellectual Property (IP): Creations of the mind like inventions, literary and artistic works, designs, symbols, names, and images used in commerce.

- Inventory: The goods and materials that a business holds for the ultimate purpose of resale.

- Internet Of Things (IoT): A network of physical objects or devices ("smart objects") connected to the internet, capable of collecting, exchanging, and acting on data. Equipped with sensors and software, these devices communicate with each other and provide real-time data.

K

- Key Performance Indicators (KPIs): Quantitative metrics used to assess a company's progress toward its business goals and identify areas for improvements. KPIs track performance over time and may focus on areas such as sales, operational efficiency, or customer satisfaction.

L

- Liability: A company's legal debts or obligations that arise during the course of business operations.

- Licensing: A business arrangement in which one company gives another company permission to manufacture its product for a specified payment.

- Limited Liability Company (LLC): A flexible form of enterprise that blends elements of partnership and corporate structures, offering limited liability to its owners.

M

- Marketing: The process of promoting and selling products or services, encompassing market research, advertising, and customer engagement strategies.

- Margin: The difference between a product's selling price and its production cost, representing the profit per unit sold.

N

- Net Income: The remaining profit of a company after deducting all expenses, including taxes, from total revenue.

O

- Organic Marketing: Also known as inbound marketing, organic marketing uses strategies that naturally attract and engage customers. Examples include content marketing, search engine optimization (SEO), and social media engagement, without relying on paid promotions.

P

- Privacy Policy: A legal document outlining how a party collects, uses, discloses, and manages a customer or client data.

R

- Return on Investment (ROI): A financial metric used to assess the profitability or efficiency of an investment, expressed as a percentage of the initial cost.

S

- S Corporation (S-Corp): A form of corporation that meets specific Internal Revenue Code requirements, giving a corporation with 100 shareholders or less the benefit of incorporation while being taxed as a partnership.

- SEM (Search Engine Marketing): A digital marketing strategy that increases websites visibility in search engine results through paid advertising. SEM tactics include pay-per-click (PPC) campaigns and keyword bidding for immediate and targeted reach.

- SEO (Search Engine Optimization): The process of optimizing a website and its content to increase visibility in organic (non-paid) search engine results. This includes incorporating relevant keywords, improving site performance, and building high-quality backlinks to enhance search engine rankings.

- Sole Proprietorship: A business structure owned and operated by one individual, with no legal distinction between the owner and the business.

- Securities: Financial instruments that represent ownership positions, creditor relationships, or rights to ownership.

T

- Terms and Conditions: A set of rules and conditions that users must agree to follow to access and use a service.

- Terms of Use: Legal agreements between a service provider and a person who wants to use that service which a user must agree to abide by in order to use a website or service.

- Trademark: A legally registered symbol, word, or phrase representing a company or product, distinguishing it from competitors.

- Term Sheet: A preliminary, non-binding document outlining the key terms and conditions of a proposed investment agreement.

www.ingramcontent.com/pod-product-compliance
Lightning Source LLC
Chambersburg PA
CBHW060317200326
41519CB00011BA/1756